COOKING WITH FRESH HERBS

Lou Seibert Pappas

BRISTOL PUBLISHING ENTERPRISES
San Leandro, California

a nitty gritty® cookbook

ISBN 1-55867-192-7

Cover design: Frank J. Paredes
Cover photography: John A. Benson
Illustrations: Shanti Nelson

CONTENTS

ALL ABOUT FRESH HERBS

Since the dawn of civilization, herbs have been used to enliven and enhance foods. Tablets, frescoes and other records testify to a very early knowledge of herb cultivation in Egypt, China, India, Arabia, Persia and Greece. Herbs were also involved medicinally in healing and in uplifting the aroma of the habitat.

Herbs are defined as the fragrant leaves of various annual or perennial plants and, sometimes, the stem of a nonwoody plant. Herbs generally come from temperate climates and their cultivation has always been a peaceful enterprise.

With their aromatic scents and distinctive flavors, fresh herbs tantalize the palate. Today, herbs are more accessible to the cook than ever before. Bunches of herbs are filling farmers' markets, gourmet shops and supermarkets with a heady fragrance, plus backyard herb gardens are springing up, handy for plucking at a moment's whim.

A wide range of reliable seeds and plants are available for sowing in home gardens. Garden plots or pots offer a rewarding combination of beauty and usefulness. Pots of lavender and lemon grass and plantings of rosemary, sage, thyme, tarragon and various-flavored mints and chives in a kitchen garden can augment the marketplace selections. Having herbs handy at our fingertips year-round means instant availability for enhancing appetizers to desserts. Plus, the surplus can be turned into vinegars, butters and pestos, or even dried, for out-of-season pleasure.

LENDING PIZZAZZ WITH FRESH HERBS

Fresh herbs lend exciting nuances to dishes, bonding with foods to create new flavor dimensions. The sheer pleasure of taste alone is reason enough for the amazing surge of herb cookery, yet our increased awareness of healthy dining also prompts this interest. Being natural flavor enhancers, herbs easily replace high caloric sauces, sweeteners and salt. What's more, replacing a classic herb with another in a favorite appetizer, salad or entrée introduces a brand new taste-treat. As world-wide travel escalates, our palates are tempted to become even more adventuresome and once overlooked herbs, such as lavender, lemon balm and lemon grass, sneak into daily fare. For example:

- Tabbouleh is a wonderful, Middle Eastern bulgur wheat salad usually containing mint. You'll discover an exciting new flavor and aroma if you substitute basil.

- With pungent basil, cherry tomatoes, cucumbers and olives make a fine accompaniment; add shrimp to become a full-meal entrée plate.

- With mint and lemon grass for seasoning, fresh fruit, such as grapes, strawberries and kiwi fruit, are delightful companions.

- Parsley makes a fanciful salad tossed with arugula, tarragon and chives in an olive oil vinaigrette, as it did in a Paris bistro. There it was paired with grilled ahi tuna.

- A superb enhancement for roasted new potatoes or sliced bakers is fresh rosemary and soft, squishy roasted garlic. This duo of rosemary and garlic ideally flavors whole wheat bread or focaccia, or use it to paint an herb glaze on egg bread.

- Pesto is a love of a summer sauce, ideal for pasta, sliced tomatoes, ratatouille, green beans and a summer squash bisque. Don't forget about substituting another herb or sun-dried tomatoes in a basil pesto for a superb stand-in.

- Mint uplifts a fish salad, perhaps stuffing big red tomatoes, cut open petal-fashion like a flower. It's a trick copied from the Greek islands where these seafood salads were among the fare at the canopy-topped cafés set up in the sand near the surfers.

- Lavender blossoms in the garden are worthy of snipping when the purple blossoms are just begin to open. Augment a sauce for roasted chicken, lace a fish sauce or perfume a citrus sorbet with fresh lavender for an aromatic surprise.

- Dill, mint and chives cleverly flavor yogurt cheese. Mint leaves can also be painted with chocolate for a "chocolate leaf" garnish next to mint ice cream.

Discover many more delectable ways to savor the fresh herb bounty in the pages that follow.

BUYING, STORING AND USING FRESH HERBS

When buying or clipping fresh herbs, choose bunches that have a clean, fresh fragrance and a bright color without any signs of wilting or browning. Seal purchased or harvested herbs in a plastic bag with a paper towel to catch any moisture and refrigerate them if you expect to use the entire supply in a day or two.

To keep them at their best for a few days or longer, herbs require special care. Leafy herbs, such as basil, cilantro, sage, lemon balm, mint and flat-leaf parsley, are best loosely tied in a bunch like a bouquet and plunged into a large canning jar with a metal clamp and a rubber ring. A 1.5 liter jar is ideal. Fill the jar with 1 inch of fresh cold tap water so the stem ends are covered. Close the jar so it is airtight and place it upright in the refrigerator. Optionally, use a jar covered with a plastic bag and secured with a rubber band. Change the water every 2 or 3 days. The herbs will keep for 7 to 10 days, far longer than if simply stored in a bag.

Some herbs with woody stems, such as thyme, oregano and rosemary, can be wrapped in a paper towel, placed in a plastic bag and kept for up to 5 days. Note that certain herbs have longer keeping qualities than others.

Dried herbs are used differently in cooking than fresh herbs, and, as a general rule, are usually 3 to 4 times more potent than fresh. Dried herbs tend to be added early in the cooking process and can withstand higher temperatures.

Fresh herbs are generally added at the end of the cooking period so that their flavors, which come from volatile aromatic oils, will be retained.

Each herb needs individual consideration as they vary in their effectiveness. Rosemary and tarragon, for example, should be used sparingly, as their flavors diffuse quickly throughout dishes. Fresh cilantro and basil produce the best flavor when added to the dish at the very last minute.

To cut leafy herbs, such as basil, lemon balm, mint, sage or sorrel, into slivers (*chiffonade*), stack a few leaves on top of each other. Roll the leaves into a tight roll from stem to tip and chop crosswise into fine strips.

To chop or mince leafy herbs, such as basil, chervil, cilantro, dill, fennel, lemon balm, marjoram, mint, parsley, sage, sorrel and tarragon, separate the leaves from the stems and place the leaves on a cutting board. Use a large knife with the point held steady. Move the knife in an up-and-down motion to cut the leaves into small pieces, changing the angle of the knife on the board often.

To use woody herbs, such as marjoram, oregano, rosemary and thyme, pluck the leaves from the woody stems with your fingers. Or, grasp one end of a stem with one hand and run the fingers of the other hand down the length of the stem to strip the leaves. Cut the leaves into smaller pieces on a cutting board with a knife if desired.

Other herbs, such as chives, lavender and lemon grass, require special treatment. Consult the *Herb Glossary*, page 6, for specific instructions.

HERB GLOSSARY

BASIL: This annual has a pungent, sweet-spicy flavor and is a member of the mint family. A key herb in Mediterranean cooking, basil plays a prominent role in the cuisines of Italy, southern France, Spain, Greece and the Middle East. There are over 40 types of basil from which to choose. The main types are *common* or *sweet basil*, *Italian basil*, *cinnamon basil*, *dwarf basil* and *opal* or *purple-leaf basil*. Basil is best added to hot dishes just before serving to retain its aromatic flavor. When possible in salads, the leaves should be torn rather than chopped to preserve the flavor.

CHERVIL: A hardy annual, chervil is one of the main ingredients in *fines herbes*. Essential in French cooking, chervil often takes the place of parsley. Its delicate flavor is diminished when heated, so add it at the end of cooking time. Chervil's feathery leaves are excellent in salads.

CHIVES: Related to the onion and leek, this fragrant herb is available year-round. It is easy to grow in pots or in the garden where its clumps produce slender vivid green tubular stems with lavender pompom flowers, which are also edible. Chives are prized as a garnish in sauces, soups and omelets. *Garlic chives* have flatter leaves and a grayer color than common chives. Their flavor has mild garlic overtones. To use, snip chives into small pieces with scissors, or mince them with a knife on a cutting board.

CILANTRO: Native to the Mediterranean and the Far East, this annual is related to the parsley family. Its fresh grass-green lacy leaves are commonly known as cilantro, Chinese parsley and fresh coriander, while its dried seeds go by the name coriander. The flavors of the seeds and leaves bear no resemblance to each other. The leaves are widely used in the cuisines of Mexico, India, Asia and the Caribbean. Americans and Europeans often find cilantro an acquired taste.

DILL: Both its fine feathery leaves and its seeds are used in the kitchen, though each has a distinctive taste. Scandinavians, Germans and Eastern and Central Europeans integrate dill into fish and egg dishes, pickles, yogurt and sour cream. Dill is essential to the famous Swedish pickled salmon dish, *gravlax*, and it enhances vegetables and seafood. Dill was well known to the ancient world where it was used medicinally and was an ingredient in many magic potions. Dried dill leaves are sold as dill weed.

FENNEL: The ancient Romans were fond of fennel in all its forms: the feathery herb, the oval-shaped seeds and the bulbous vegetable. Native to southern Europe, the fennel plant resembles dill, but grows about twice as tall. There are two main types. *Florence fennel* has a distinct anise flavor. Its broad base is treated as a vegetable, while its feathery leaves are used as an herb. *Common fennel* produces fennel seeds. The Italians favor fennel with pork, veal, soups, salads and fish.

LAVENDER: This relative of mint was once widely used to flavor wines, teas and sweets. It was also prized for centuries to calm nerves and refresh linens. Today lavender is regaining a culinary niche in enhancing sorbets, ice creams and custards. This biennial makes an excellent landscape plant, as it is easy to grow, virtually pest-free and drought-tolerant once established. Lavender's scented flowers offer a double option, as a decorative item or culinary ingredient. To use, strip the flowers from the stems. If growing in your garden, do not harvest too far in advance.

LEMON BALM: This easily grown and propagated plant has light green leaves that taste and smell of sweet lemon. Once stripped from their stems, the leaves are excellent chopped and incorporated into salads, soups, egg dishes, tea and fish.

LEMON GRASS: An important flavoring in Thai, Vietnamese and other Southeast Asian cooking, lemon grass thrives in tropical climates. It can also be grown in temperate zones. Lemon grass is characterized by long spear-like fibrous leaves and a bulbous base. To use, peel off the outer fibrous portion of the stalk and chop finely. Use only the lower 4 to 6 inches, discarding the tough upper part. Lemon grass's citrusy, slightly gingery flavor enhances curries, soups, stews and casseroles, particularly those composed of chicken or seafood. If unavailable, fresh lemon peel (zest) and a bit of grated fresh ginger can stand in.

MARJORAM: There are many species of this ancient herb, which is found throughout the Mediterranean. Marjoram is used extensively in meat and poultry dishes, stuffings, sausages and pizzas. Its flavor is delicate and dissipates readily; add it at the end of cooking.

MINT: There are a vast number of mints, yet all share the cool aromatic taste of *menthol*. *Spearmint*, *apple mint* and *peppermint* are the three most commonly cultivated for culinary purposes. Others include *lemon-flavored mint*, *pineapple mint*, *eau de Cologne* and *pennyroyal*. Fresh mint is popular with iced tea, lamb dishes and fruit salads, and is indispensable in mint julep cocktails. Mint is best if used fresh and stored briefly.

OREGANO: Sometimes called wild marjoram, oregano belongs to the mint family and is related to both marjoram and thyme. Though similar to marjoram, it is not as sweet and has a stronger, pungent flavor and aroma. It is popularly enjoyed in Mediterranean meat and poultry dishes, and with pastas, pizzas, beans and seafood.

PARSLEY: Of the many varieties of this popular herb, the two main ones are *curly-leaf*, a decorative variety, and *flat-leaf* or *Italian*, ideal for cooking and eating. In medicinal folklore, parsley is touted as a cure for rheumatism and lethargy. With its peppery bite and hints of camphor, citrus and grass, parsley cleans and refreshes. It is often used to bring out the flavor of other herbs and is always included in *bouquet garni* and *fines herbes* mixtures. Parsley is good with nearly every type of food.

ROSEMARY: Its needle-shaped evergreen leaves have a potent pine and lemon scent that easily seasons a variety of dishes. Use rosemary with discretion, as it is a powerful herb. Rosemary is especially effective baked in breads or used in marinades with lamb, pork and chicken. Rosemary grows wild throughout the Mediterranean. The Italians make great use of rosemary by sprinkling it on focaccia and burning branches of it under grilled fish and meats to impart flavor.

SAGE: Fresh sage is vastly superior to its dried form. Sage's pungent, aromatic camphor taste, popular in Italy, enhances poultry stuffings, sausage, veal, pork, risottos, beans and tomato-based sauces. The leaves are good threaded between cubes of meat or vegetables when preparing kebabs. Sage has been used for centuries for both culinary and medicinal purposes.

SORREL: *Garden sorrel* and *French sorrel* are two allied species, notable for their acidic or sour flavor. Sorrel's high acidity causes it to discolor when it is cooked in iron pots, or when it is chopped with knives other than stainless steel. Sorrel enjoys its greatest popularity in France, where it is integrated into soups, fish, veal and egg dishes. Because of its acidity, sorrel acts as a meat tenderizer.

TARRAGON: With its sophisticated anise-like flavor, tarragon is a staple in classic French sauces, and in chicken, fish, vegetable and egg dishes. Tarragon-flavored wine vinegar is a popular item in gourmet markets. Tarragon should be used sparingly, as its flavor diffuses quickly throughout dishes. There are 2 types of tarragon. *French tarragon* is favored for its delicate flavor. *Russian tarragon* has a more pungent, slightly bitter taste.

THYME: This perennial herb comes in several varieties, such as *garden thyme* and *lemon thyme*. Garden thyme is most favored for cooking and has a strong, slightly bitter flavor due to the volatile oil *thymol*. It is one of the most important culinary herbs of Europe, widely used in Mediterranean countries and especially in the French kitchen. Lemon thyme, a popular variety, is often preferred with fish and egg dishes and baked sweets. Thyme is reputed to enhance the memory. It goes well with meats and fish, and is often incorporated into herb butters, stuffings, soups, potatoes and bean dishes.

HERB COMBINATIONS: Certain herbs and foods have an affinity for each other: fennel for fish; basil for tomatoes and eggplant; oregano for beans; rosemary for lamb; sage for pork; and tarragon for eggs. Certain combinations of herbs also go well together. A fresh *bouquet garni* (herb bundle) consists of 3 sprigs parsley, 1 sprig thyme and 1 bay leaf tied together with kitchen string with a small celery stalk or the green part of a leek. Let it simmer in a soup pot or with a sauce. The formula can be varied by including fennel or dill to flavor a fish stock or sauce.

DIPS, SPREADS AND ACCOMPANIMENTS

SPINACH-JICAMA DIP

Makes about 2½ cups

This popular dip can easily be served in a hollowed-out 1-pound round loaf of French bread. Or, use small 6-inch-round crusty breads if you wish.

1 bunch (12 oz.) fresh spinach, stems removed, chopped, or 1 pkg. (10 oz.) frozen chopped spinach, thawed
½ cup (4 oz.) low-fat sour cream
½ cup plain yogurt
1 tsp. balsamic vinegar
3 green onions, with green tops, finely chopped
2 tsp. lemon juice

⅛ tsp. nutmeg
⅓ cup chopped jicama or sliced water chestnuts
¼ cup finely minced fresh flat-leaf parsley
salt and pepper to taste
crackers, raw sliced zucchini or carrots for dippers, optional
1 lb. round French bread, optional

In a large skillet, cook spinach over high heat just until limp, about 2 minutes. Drain spinach well and squeeze dry; cool. In a large bowl, mix sour cream, yogurt, vinegar, onions, lemon juice, nutmeg, jicama, parsley and spinach. Season with salt and pepper. Spoon into a serving container, cover and chill for 1 hour. Serve with dippers, or if desired, hollow out French bread, leaving a ¼-inch wall. Tear soft inside bread into cubes for dipping.

INDIAN CARROT DIP
WITH BASIL PESTO

Makes about 2½ cups

Striking colors and flavors produce this winning appetizer that is easy to make in advance and tote to a party.

1 small onion, chopped
4 medium carrots, sliced
¼ cup water
⅓ cup orange juice
peel (zest) of 1 orange, finely slivered
⅛ tsp. salt
⅛ tsp. freshly ground pepper

1 tsp. curry powder
1 tbs. minced fresh ginger
2 tbs. plain yogurt
1 tbs. stone-ground mustard
about ⅓ cup *Basil Pesto*, page 21
basil blossoms for garnish, optional
stone-ground crackers

Place onion, carrots and water in a saucepan. Cover and simmer for 7 minutes. Add orange juice, orange peel, salt, pepper, curry powder and ginger and simmer for 10 to 15 minutes, or until vegetables are tender and juices are evaporated. Transfer to a food processor workbowl, add yogurt and mustard and puree until smooth. Transfer mixture to a bowl, cover and chill for several hours.

At serving time, spoon *Basil Pesto* into center of dip. Garnish with basil blossoms, if using, and accompany with crackers.

EGGPLANT-SUNFLOWER SEED SPREAD

Makes about 3 cups

An herb-sparked eggplant spread can serve as an appetizer with crackers, or offer it as a first course, ringing it with small red and gold plum tomatoes.

1 large eggplant, about 1¼ lb.
¼ lb. shiitake mushrooms, stemmed and chopped, or white mushrooms, chopped
2 shallots, chopped
1 tbs. olive oil
2 tbs. lemon juice
3 cloves garlic, minced

salt and freshly ground pepper to taste
⅓ cup plain yogurt
2 tbs. minced fresh basil
3 tbs. minced fresh flat-leaf parsley
romaine lettuce leaves
¼ cup sunflower kernels, toasted
niçoise olives for garnish, optional
crisp lavosh or sesame crackers

Heat oven to 400°. Bake whole eggplant in a baking pan uncovered for 30 to 40 minutes, or until soft. Dip into cold water. Prick eggplant with a fork and squeeze out juices; peel and cool. Puree eggplant flesh with a food processor or blender. In a small skillet over medium-high heat, sauté mushrooms and shallots in oil until softened, about 2 minutes, and add to eggplant. Puree with lemon juice and garlic. Season with salt and pepper and stir in yogurt, basil and parsley. Transfer to a container, cover and chill.

At serving time, mound spread on a plate lined with romaine and sprinkle with sunflower kernels. Ring with olives, if using. Accompany with crackers.

TOMATO AND BASIL CHEESE SPREAD

Makes about 1½ cups

Sun-dried tomatoes, basil and garlic enliven this spread to top toasted baguettes, raw vegetables or baked potatoes. Or, dollop on broiled fish.

1 cup *Yogurt Cheese*, follows
⅓ cup snipped oil-packed sun-dried
   tomatoes
2 cloves garlic, minced
2 tbs. minced fresh basil

1 tbs. minced fresh chives or green
   onion tops
dash salt
freshly ground pepper to taste

In a bowl, mix *Yogurt Cheese* with tomatoes, garlic, basil, chives, salt and pepper. Cover and chill for 2 hours to blend flavors. Serve at room temperature.

YOGURT CHEESE

Makes about 1 cup

2 cups low-fat gelatin-free yogurt

Place yogurt in a yogurt strainer or a mesh strainer lined with cheesecloth and set in a bowl to catch liquid (whey). Cover and chill for 6 to 24 hours, until whey drains off and cheese is desired thickness; discard whey.

HERB-FLAVORED YOGURT CHEESE

Makes about 1½ cups

Herb-flavored yogurt cheeses tempt vacationers in Turkey at the breakfast and dinner hotel buffets throughout the countryside. This cheese makes a delicious topping on breads, salads, grains and meats. Use full-fat yogurt for an authentic richness.

3 cups plain gelatin-free yogurt
2 cloves garlic, minced
1 tbs. minced fresh dill, chives, mint,
   marjoram or tarragon
salt to taste

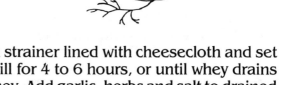

Place yogurt in a yogurt strainer or a mesh strainer lined with cheesecloth and set in a bowl to catch liquid (whey). Cover and chill for 4 to 6 hours, or until whey drains off and cheese is desired thickness; discard whey. Add garlic, herbs and salt to drained yogurt and mix until blended. Cover and chill until ready to serve.

VARIATION: CARROT-PARSLEY YOGURT CHEESE

Substitute 1 medium carrot, finely grated and steamed for 1 minute, and 2 tbs. minced fresh flat-leaf parsley for garlic and herbs.

FRUIT-CILANTRO SALSA

A versatile ginger- and cilantro-sparked fruit salsa can be made with a variety of fresh fruits.

2 cups diced mango, papaya,
  nectarines or peaches
½ cup diced red onion
½ cup diced red bell pepper
¼ cup minced fresh cilantro

2 tbs. lime juice
2 tsp. grated fresh ginger
dash chili powder, optional
Whole Wheat Tortilla Chips, follow,
  optional

In a medium bowl, place mango, red onion, red pepper, cilantro, lime juice, ginger and chili powder, if using, and mix lightly. Cover and chill until serving time. Serve as a side dish or with *Whole Wheat Tortilla Chips* as an appetizer.

WHOLE WHEAT TORTILLA CHIPS

Makes 32

Heat oven to 350°. Quickly dip 4 whole wheat tortillas in a bowl of cold water. Drain and cut each tortilla into 8 triangles. Arrange tortillas on baking pans in a single layer and bake, one pan at a time, for 10 minutes, or until chips are crisp and lightly browned.

TOMATO CHILE SALSA

This hot chile salsa makes a vibrant accent for tacos, grilled meats, chicken and fish. Vary the heat level to suit your taste.

3 firm, ripe tomatoes, peeled, seeded and chopped
1 small sweet red or white onion, finely chopped
1 small fresh jalapeño, serrano or Fresno chile, seeded and chopped,
    or 2-3 tbs. chopped canned green chiles
salt and pepper to taste
½ tsp. sugar
3 tbs. minced fresh cilantro

In a bowl, mix together tomatoes, onion, chile, salt, pepper, sugar and cilantro. Cover and chill for 1 hour to blend flavors.

SWISS HERB SAUCE

Let this zestful herb sauce drench baked potatoes, green beans, steak or grilled salmon.

¼ cup olive oil or unsalted butter
1 anchovy fillet, chopped
1 tsp. Dijon mustard
1 tsp. lemon juice
6 tbs. minced fresh flat-leaf parsley
2 shallots, finely chopped
1 clove garlic, minced
2 tsp. minced fresh chives or tarragon

In a small saucepan, heat oil, anchovy, mustard and lemon juice over medium heat until heated through. Remove from heat and stir in parsley, shallots, garlic and chives. Spoon warm sauce over vegetables, meats or fish.

BASIL PESTO

This classic sauce has a wealth of uses: toss it with pasta, spoon it over vegetables or grilled seafood, or blend it into yogurt and sour cream for a fast dip.

2 cups fresh basil leaves, packed
3 tbs. pine nuts or pistachio nuts
2 large cloves garlic
¼ cup extra virgin olive oil
3 tbs. freshly grated Reggiano
   Parmesan cheese

With a food processor, process basil, nuts and garlic until finely minced. Add oil and cheese and process until mixed. Transfer to a small bowl, cover and chill.

OREGANO PESTO

Makes about ¾ cup

This is a wonderful all-purpose pesto that retains its lovely verdant green color. Try this on summer squash and roasted eggplant slices, onion rings, red peppers or new potatoes. It is also good with lentil or black bean soup, grilled lamb chops or roasted chicken.

⅓ cup fresh oregano leaves, packed
1 cup fresh flat-leaf parsley leaves, packed
¾ cup fresh spinach leaves, packed
2 tbs. walnuts or pistachio nuts, toasted
1 large clove garlic, smashed
3 tbs. olive oil
3 tbs. grated Parmesan or Romano cheese

With a food processor, process oregano, parsley, spinach, nuts and garlic until finely minced. Add oil and cheese and process until mixed. Transfer to a small bowl, cover and chill.

SUN-DRIED TOMATO AND ROASTED GARLIC PESTO

This luscious spread explodes with wonderful herb and nut flavors. Accompany it with a basket of breads for an appetizer or serve it as a tableside meal accompaniment.

1 cup dried sun-dried tomatoes
1/3 cup water
3 tbs. roasted garlic puree
1/3 cup fresh flat-leaf parsley leaves, packed
1/4 cup fresh basil leaves, packed
1 green onion, chopped
2 tbs. pistachio nuts
3 tbs. grated Parmesan or Romano cheese
sliced baguette and assorted crusty breads

Place tomatoes in a small saucepan with water and simmer over low heat for 5 minutes, or until softened; drain, if necessary, and cool. With a food processor, process garlic puree, tomatoes, parsley, basil, onion and nuts until finely minced. Add cheese and process until mixed. Transfer to a small bowl, cover and chill. Serve with sliced breads.

NOTE: Roasted garlic puree is available commercially in jars. Or, to make your own, heat oven to 350°. Slice off the top 1/4 inch of 1 whole bulb garlic and place in a small baking dish; rub bulb with 2 tsp. olive oil. Bake for 30 to 35 minutes, or until soft. When cool, squeeze soft garlic pulp from its papery wrapper into a bowl.

HERB BUTTERS

Unsalted butter can be flavored variously with herbs to dollop over hot meats or fish or to spread on tea sandwiches.

¼ lb. unsalted butter, room temperature
3-4 tbs. minced fresh chives, parsley, chervil, dill,
    marjoram, sorrel, thyme, tarragon or basil
2 tbs. lemon juice
1 clove garlic, minced, optional

In a bowl or with a food processor, blend butter with herbs, lemon juice and garlic, if using. Shape into a cylinder and wrap with plastic wrap or pack into a container; cover and chill.

At serving time, slice flavored butter into rounds or spoon out and dollop onto hot foods. Or, bring to room temperature and use as a spread for sandwiches.

HERB VINEGARS

Herb-flavored vinegars can be prepared with most any culinary herb. Try rosemary for lamb and meat dishes; tarragon for salads and chicken dishes; dill or fennel for fish and potato dishes; sage for meat marinades; and lemon balm or mint for fruit salads or desserts. Perhaps the most versatile vinegar to use is white wine vinegar for its pleasing taste and absence of color. Cider vinegar, red wine vinegar or rice wine vinegar are also appropriate. Use the following mixed herbal vinegar for salads with a zesty blue or Parmesan cheese, or in a marinade for red meats.

2 sprigs fresh rosemary, plus more for garnish, optional

3 sprigs fresh oregano or marjoram, plus more for garnish, optional

2 sprigs fresh sage, plus more for garnish, optional

2 sprigs fresh flat-leaf parsley or chervil, plus more for garnish, optional

1 clove garlic

2 tsp. black peppercorns

1 qt. red wine vinegar

Place herb sprigs, garlic and peppercorns in a sterilized bottle and add vinegar. Cap and place in a sunny window for 2 weeks. Use immediately, or for longer storage, strain through a coffee filter into a clean bottle and add 1 to 2 sprigs fresh herbs. Seal well.

Optionally, heat vinegar to boiling, pour over herb mixture and let stand until cool; strain and transfer to a clean bottle with 1 to 2 sprigs fresh herbs. Seal well.

APPETIZERS

MARINATED HERBED CHEESE

Fresh mixed herbs steep in olive oil with chunks of cheese for an ultra-simple, make-ahead appetizer. Packed in a wide-mouthed jar, the cheese travels with ease to a picnic or outdoor gathering.

8 oz. Jarlsberg or Monterey Jack cheese
2 tbs. mixed fresh herbs, such as thyme, oregano,
    marjoram, tarragon, chives, sage and/or rosemary
1 dried hot red chile, split, optional
1 bay leaf
about ¾ cup extra virgin olive oil
sesame crackers or a thinly sliced baguette
vegetable accompaniments: fennel stalks, sliced
    mushrooms, sliced zucchini, red
    bell pepper strips and/or jicama sticks

Cut cheese into 1¼-inch cubes and place in a wide-mouthed jar. Sprinkle with herbs. Add chile, if using, and bay leaf. Pour in oil to just cover cheese. Cover and chill for at least 3 to 4 days. Accompany with crackers or sliced baguette and a tray of vegetables.

SAVORY HERB AND CHEESE BISCOTTI

Imbued with garlic, Parmesan and herbs, these crispy biscotti are perfect with wine or for all-around snacking.

6 tbs. dry sun-dried tomato halves
1/4 cup water
1/2 cup butter, softened
2 tbs. tomato paste
1 cup (4 oz.) grated Parmesan cheese
2 eggs
3 cloves garlic, minced
1 tbs. minced fresh rosemary
1 tbs. minced fresh oregano
1 1/2 tsp. baking powder
1/2 tsp. salt
1/4 tsp. freshly ground pepper
2 cups plus 2 tbs. unbleached all-purpose flour
3/4 cup pistachio nuts

Heat oven to 350°. In a small saucepan, place tomatoes and water, cover and simmer over low heat for 2 minutes; cool. In a large bowl, beat butter, tomato paste and cheese until blended. Add eggs one at a time, beating well after each addition, and stir in garlic, herbs and 1 tbs. of the tomato-soaking liquid. Stir together baking powder, salt and flour, add to egg mixture and beat just until smooth. Drain tomatoes well and chop finely. Mix in tomatoes and nuts until well distributed. Divide dough in half and shape into 2 logs, about 2½ inches wide, ⅞-inch thick and 14 inches long on a parchment-lined or buttered and floured baking sheet. Pat logs smooth on top. Bake for 30 minutes, or until firm and lightly browned on edges.

Remove logs from oven and cool for 20 minutes. Transfer logs to a cutting board and cut on the diagonal into ⅜-inch-wide slices with a serrated knife. Return to baking sheet, flat-side down. Reduce oven heat to 300° and bake for 20 minutes, turning halfway through baking time. Cool completely and store in an airtight container.

LAVOSH PINWHEELS WITH VEGETABLES

Lavosh (Armenian cracker bread) gains a vegetarian filling for a decorative pinwheel sandwich. Serve this as a generous appetizer or a light luncheon entrée. If softened lavosh is available, omit the moistening step.

1 large round lavosh
1 cup *Yogurt Cheese*, page 16, or
   whipped light cream cheese
1 tsp. balsamic vinegar
about 6 outer leaves romaine lettuce,
   center ribs removed, or other greens,
   such as arugula or red mustard
3 carrots, shredded

1 cucumber, peeled and thinly sliced,
   about 1½ cups
1 cup alfalfa sprouts
2½ cups broccoli florets, cooked until
   tender-crisp and chopped
2 tbs. minced fresh flat-leaf parsley,
   chervil or dill
2 tbs. minced fresh garlic chives

Dampen 1 large or 2 small kitchen towels and wring out excess moisture. Moisten lavosh well on both sides under cold running water. Place lavosh darker-side down between layers of damp towel and set aside until soft and pliable, about 45 minutes.

Remove top towel. Mix *Yogurt Cheese* with vinegar and spread over lavosh. Cover with greens and top with vegetables, stopping about 4 inches from the far edge. Sprinkle with herbs. Fold an inch or so of the near edge over filling, lift bottom towel and roll lavosh gently but firmly, jelly roll-fashion. Wrap roll with plastic wrap and chill for 1 to 24 hours. At serving time, cut into ¾-inch round slices.

ROASTED YAM SLICES
WITH SAUSAGES AND SAGE

Golden discs of crunchy yams topped with smoky light-style sausage and herbs create a tasty starter. Choose one of the many low-fat sausages, such as chicken-apple or turkey-cranberry.

2-3 medium yams, preferably long and skinny
olive oil
3 low-fat sausages, such as chicken-apple
   or turkey-cranberry
fresh sage, basil or lemon balm leaves for garnish

Heat oven to 400°. Scrub yams well and peel. Cut peeled yams into 1/4-inch-thick round slices. Lightly coat a large baking sheet with nonstick cooking spray or olive oil. Arrange yam slices in 1 layer and brush with oil. Bake slices for 30 minutes, turning once or twice. Cut sausages into 1/4-inch-thick round slices and place on another baking sheet. Reduce oven heat to 350° and bake yams and sausages for 10 minutes, or until yams are cooked through and slightly crisp and sausages are heated through. Top each yam slice with a sausage slice and garnish with herb leaves.

ROASTED NEW POTATOES IN VARIATION

New potatoes oven-roast to a caramelized sheen and flavor, ready to halve or hollow and top with a complimentary accent.

12 small red Bliss potatoes or red-skinned new potatoes
1 tbs. extra virgin olive oil
1 tbs. balsamic vinegar
salt and freshly ground pepper to taste
assorted *Toppings*, follow

Heat oven to 475°. Halve potatoes and toss with oil and vinegar; let stand for a few minutes and season with salt and pepper. Place potatoes in a single layer on a baking sheet and roast for 20 to 25 minutes, turning once or twice, until tender. Serve with one or more *Toppings*.

TOPPINGS

CHIVE OR DILL YOGURT CHEESE: Blend ½ cup *Yogurt Cheese*, page 16, with 1 clove minced garlic and 2 tbs. minced fresh chives or dill.

HERBS AND GOAT CHEESE: Blend 2 oz. goat cheese with 2 tbs. minced fresh thyme, oregano, marjoram, chervil or flat-leaf parsley.

SOUR CREAM, CAVIAR AND CHIVES: Top potatoes with ½ cup sour cream and 3 tbs. red or black caviar; sprinkle with 1 tbs. minced fresh chives or dill.

GALETTES WITH TOMATOES AND GOAT CHEESE

In Brittany, crepes made with buckwheat flour are a delicious discovery in the charming creperies that dot the area. The fillings are numerous and varied. Here is a favorite California interpretation. The crepes can be made in advance and refrigerated. Look for buckwheat flour in health food or specialty food stores, often in the bulk bins.

CREPES

2 eggs
¾ cup milk
¼ cup buckwheat flour
⅓ cup unbleached all-purpose flour
1 tbs. cassis (black currant) syrup
butter

TOPPING

4 oz. goat cheese
1 cup oil-packed sun-dried tomatoes
⅓ cup minced fresh basil

For crepes, process eggs, milk, flours and cassis syrup with a food processor or blender until smooth. Transfer batter to a bowl, cover and chill for 1 hour.

Heat a 6- or 7-inch crepe pan or small nonstick skillet over medium-high heat. Add butter just to coat pan. Stir batter, ladle 2 tbs. of the batter into pan and swirl to coat the bottom of pan evenly. Cook for about 1 minute, or until the bottom of crepe is browned; turn and cook the opposite side for about 15 seconds. Transfer crepe to a platter and repeat the cooking process with remaining batter, buttering pan when necessary. Stack finished crepes.

Heat oven to 375°. Lay 4 crepes browned-side down on a work surface. Spread half of each crepe with goat cheese and scatter tomatoes and basil over cheese. Fold crepes in half to cover filling. Place filled crepes on an ovenproof platter. If desired, assemble crepes to this point and chill, covered, for 4 to 6 hours. Bake crepes for 5 minutes (15 minutes, if refrigerated), or until heated through.

VARIATION: BLINI WITH SMOKED SALMON

With a food processor, blend ¾ cup low-fat cottage cheese with ¼ cup light-style sour cream; stir in 3 tbs. minced fresh chives. Spread mixture on cooked crepes and top with 3 oz. smoked salmon, cut into strips. Fold in half and serve.

MUSHROOM HAZELNUT PATÉ

Mushrooms lend a wonderful meaty character to this flavor-packed paté.

¼ cup hazelnuts or walnuts
2 tbs. olive oil
2 shallots, finely chopped
½ lb. shiitake mushrooms or white
    mushrooms, chopped
1 clove garlic, minced
2 tsp. lemon juice
1 tbs. minced fresh tarragon

salt and pepper to taste
1 tbs. balsamic vinegar
3 tbs. minced fresh flat-leaf parsley
2 tbs. plain yogurt
2 tbs. grated Parmesan cheese
flat-leaf parsley sprigs or chive
    blossoms for garnish
sesame crackers or crisp lavosh

Heat oven to 325°. Spread hazelnuts in a shallow pan and bake for 8 to 10 minutes, or until lightly toasted. Rub nuts between paper towels to remove as much of the skins as possible; cool nuts and chop finely. In a large skillet, heat oil over medium heat, add shallots and sauté for 2 to 3 minutes. Add mushrooms, garlic and lemon juice and cook until glazed. Transfer to a bowl and mix in tarragon, salt and pepper. Cook any remaining pan juices with vinegar until reduced to a glaze and spoon over mushroom mixture. Add nuts, parsley, yogurt and cheese and process until nearly smooth with a food processor. Spoon into a serving container, cover and chill for 2 hours or longer to blend flavors. Garnish with parsley sprigs and serve with crackers.

WILD MUSHROOM PARTY PATÉ

A medley of mushrooms lends a beguiling flavor to this neat-to-slice vegetable paté. A combination of brown domestic mushrooms, stemmed shiitake mushrooms and porcini mushrooms works well.

2 leeks, white part only, finely chopped
⅓ cup chopped celery
2 tbs. olive oil
1 lb. mixed domestic and wild
   mushrooms
3 oz. Neufchatel cheese, or ⅓ cup
   Yogurt Cheese, page 16

2 eggs, lightly beaten
salt and freshly ground pepper to taste
2 tbs. minced fresh basil or tarragon
¾ cup fine dry breadcrumbs
fresh basil, parsley or chervil sprigs for
   garnish

Heat oven to 325°. In a skillet, sauté leeks and celery in oil over medium-high heat for 5 to 7 minutes, or until soft. Add mushrooms and sauté until glazed; remove from heat. In a large bowl, combine cheese, eggs, salt, pepper and basil. Add mushroom mixture and breadcrumbs and mix well. Transfer to an oiled 9-x-5-inch loaf pan. Place a strip of waxed paper on top and cover with aluminum foil. Bake for 1 hour, or until set. Cool to room temperature and chill.

At serving time, invert paté onto a serving platter and slice. Garnish with herb sprigs.

BAKED MUSHROOMS WITH CHÈVRE

Big plump mushroom caps make savory containers for a softly oozing herb-flavored cheese stuffing.

⅔ lb. large white, shiitake or small portobello
   mushrooms, about 2-2½ inches in diameter
1 tbs. butter
1 tbs. olive oil
¼ cup minced fresh flat-leaf parsley or chervil
1 tbs. chopped fresh tarragon
2 cloves garlic, minced
4 oz. chèvre (soft goat cheese), cut into 4 slices
2 oz. prosciutto or ham, thinly sliced, optional

Heat oven to 425°. Separate mushroom stems from caps. Slice each cap into 4 to 5 slices, keeping slices together so that they retain the shape of whole mushroom. Arrange caps cup-side up in 4 small baking dishes. In a small saucepan, melt butter with oil and mix in parsley, tarragon and garlic. Drizzle butter mixture over mushrooms and bake for 5 minutes. Arrange a slice each of cheese and prosciutto, if using, on top of each dish and continue baking for about 5 minutes, until cheese melts.

CRAB-FILLED MUSHROOM CAPS

A hot seafood filling uplifts bite-sized mushroom caps for a sumptuous morsel.

1 lb. white or brown mushrooms, about
   1 inch in diameter
1 tbs. unsalted butter
1 tbs. olive oil
2 eggs
¾ cup crumbled soft French bread
3 tbs. light-style sour cream
1 cup cooked fresh crabmeat or shrimp

2 green onions, chopped
2 tbs. minced fresh marjoram, dill,
   fennel or tarragon
2 tbs. minced fresh flat-leaf parsley
   or chervil
salt and freshly ground pepper to taste
¼ cup (1 oz.) shredded Parmesan or
   Romano cheese

Heat oven to 375°. Separate mushroom stems from caps and chop stems. In a large skillet, sauté chopped mushroom stems in 1 tsp. each of the butter and oil over medium-high heat just until glazed. In a bowl, beat eggs until blended and mix in sautéed mushroom stems, bread, sour cream, crabmeat, onions, herbs, salt and pepper. In remaining butter and oil, sauté mushroom caps in skillet until glazed. Place caps cup-side up in a nonstick baking dish. Pile crab filling in each mushroom cap and sprinkle with cheese. Bake for 10 minutes, or until filling is set.

BRUSCHETTA WITH SMOKED SALMON AND GOAT CHEESE

A smear of goat cheese, a slice of smoked salmon and a wisp of fresh dill overlay crispy garlic toast for a festive appetizer.

12 slices baguette
2 cloves garlic, peeled and cut in half
extra virgin olive oil
3 oz. mild white goat cheese (chèvre)

3 oz. sliced smoked salmon
12 small sprigs dill, fennel, basil
   or watercress
freshly ground pepper to taste

Heat grill to medium high, or heat oven to 350°. Rub bread with cut side of garlic cloves and drizzle lightly with olive oil. Grill or bake bread until lightly toasted. Arrange toasted bread on a platter, spread with goat cheese and top with salmon, herbs and pepper.

VARIATION: BRUSCHETTA WITH MUSHROOMS AND HERBS

For salmon, substitute ¾ lb. sliced white mushrooms tossed with 2 tbs. olive oil, 1½ tbs. lemon juice, 1 tsp. minced fresh thyme, 1 tsp. minced fresh chives, 1 tbs. minced fresh flat-leaf parsley and salt and freshly ground pepper to taste. Spread garlic toast with goat cheese and spoon mushroom topping over the top.

COLD MARINATED TROUT

Piquant morsels of trout make a savory appetizer on toasted country bread or a handsome first course when the fish is presented whole.

4 small whole trout, about 12 oz. each
1 tsp. olive oil
4 shallots, thinly sliced
¾ cup tarragon-flavored white wine vinegar
¾ cup water
3 tbs. dry sherry

1½ tbs. pickling spice, tied in a small square of cheesecloth
small leaf lettuce
thin-sliced country bread, toasted, optional
2 tbs. minced fresh dill, fennel or tarragon for garnish

In a large skillet, sauté trout in oil over medium-high heat for 1 minute on each side. Place trout and shallots in a shallow ceramic or glass dish. In a saucepan, heat vinegar with water, sherry and pickling spices; simmer for 5 minutes. Pour hot marinade over fish and shallots. Cool, cover and chill for 2 days, basting occasionally.

Remove head, tail, skin and bones of trout. Serve fillets on toasted bread strips as an appetizer or on a bed of lettuce as a first course. Garnish with herbs.

STUFFED MUSSELS

The hinged shells of mussels or clams provide artistic serving containers for seafood pilaf. Chilled, they are an intriguing appetizer or first course; hot, they are a conversational entrée.

12 mussels, beards removed, or clams
   (little neck or rock)
½ cup dry white wine
½ cup water
salt to taste
1 large onion, finely chopped
2 tbs. olive oil
1 cup short-grain rice
3 tbs. pine nuts
⅓ cup tomato sauce
½ tsp. ground allspice
⅓ cup dried currants
2 tbs. minced fresh fennel or dill
small sprigs fresh fennel or dill for garnish
lemon wedges

With a stiff brush, scrub mussels thoroughly under cold running water. Place mussels in a saucepan, add wine and water and sprinkle lightly with salt. Cover and steam over high heat for 10 minutes, or until mussel shells open. Discard any unopened mussels and set remaining mussels aside. Strain broth into a measuring cup; if necessary, add water to yield 1½ cups liquid.

In a medium saucepan, sauté onion in oil over medium-high heat until golden. Add rice and pine nuts and sauté until nuts turn golden brown. Pour 1½ cups reserved liquid over rice mixture. Add tomato sauce, allspice and currants. Cover and bring to a boil, reduce heat to low and simmer for 12 minutes. Remove from heat and let stand for 10 minutes. Remove mussels from shells, chop coarsely and combine with rice and chopped herbs; spoon mixture into shells. Cover and chill.

To reheat, place in a steamer and steam over simmering water until heated through.

At serving time, sprinkle stuffed mussels with herb wisps and garnish with lemon wedges.

ASPARAGUS WITH SMOKED SALMON

Servings: 12 appetizer,
or 4 first course

A ribbon of smoked salmon bands fresh tender-crisp asparagus spears for a savory springtime finger food.

1 lb. fresh large asparagus spears
2 oz. whipped light-style cream cheese
  or soft goat cheese
2 tsp. minced fresh dill or chives
3 oz. smoked salmon, cut into 1/2-inch strips

Peel ends of asparagus with a vegetable peeler. Cook asparagus in a large amount of boiling salted water until tender-crisp, about 5 to 7 minutes. Drain and plunge into cold water to chill; drain again. Blend cheese with dill or chives. Spread a dollop of cheese on the center of each asparagus spear and wrap with a short strip of salmon. Arrange on a platter.

BREADS

ROASTED GARLIC AND ROSEMARY LOAVES   Makes 2 loaves

Roasted garlic studs this wholesome whole wheat bread for a savory loaf to accompany cheeses and meats. It's excellent toasted as well, served as an appetizer spread with chèvre and topped with sun-dried tomatoes.

2 pkg. active dry yeast
2½ cups lukewarm water
2 cups stone-ground whole wheat flour
about 3 cups unbleached all-purpose flour
2½ tsp. salt
3 tbs. honey
3 tbs. olive oil
2 tbs. chopped fresh rosemary
8 cloves garlic, unpeeled
1½ tsp. olive oil

In a small bowl, sprinkle yeast into ½ cup of the water and let stand until dissolved and puffy, about 10 minutes. In a bowl, place whole wheat flour, ½ cup of the all-purpose flour and salt. Add remaining water, honey and 3 tbs. olive oil and mix with a heavy duty mixer or beat with a wooden spoon until well mixed. Mix in proofed yeast and 1 tbs. of the rosemary. Gradually stir in enough of the remaining flour to make a soft dough; you may not need to use all of it. Knead with mixer's dough hook or transfer to a lightly floured board and knead by hand for 10 minutes. Place kneaded dough in a lightly oiled bowl, cover with plastic wrap and let rise until doubled in size, about 1½ hours.

Heat oven to 325°. Place garlic in a small baking dish, rub with ½ tsp. oil and bake for 30 minutes, or until soft; peel and cut into pieces. Add remaining rosemary and 1 tsp. oil, mixing lightly.

Punch down dough and transfer to a lightly floured board. Divide dough in half and shape into 2 oval loaves. Place loaves on a lightly oiled baking sheet. With a finger, poke about 8 holes in the top surface of each loaf. Fill holes with garlic and herb mixture, dividing evenly. Cover and let rise until doubled in size, about 45 to 50 minutes.

Heat oven to 375°. Brush dough surface with olive oil. Bake for 35 minutes, or until golden brown; loaves should sound hollow when thumped. Cool on a rack.

WHOLE WHEAT HAZELNUT HERB BREAD

This herb-scented nut bread is ideal for sandwiches. Or, serve slices as an accompaniment to a soup or salad meal.

2 pkg. active dry yeast
1/2 cup lukewarm water
3 tbs. honey or brown sugar
3 tbs. olive oil
2 1/2 tsp. salt
3 cups whole wheat flour
3 cups unbleached all-purpose flour
2 1/2 cups water
1/4 cup wheat germ or bran
2/3 cup toasted hazelnuts or walnuts
1/2 cup mixed minced fresh thyme, chives,
    oregano and rosemary

In a small bowl, sprinkle yeast into ½ cup water and let stand until dissolved and puffy, about 10 minutes. In a bowl, place honey, oil, salt and 1 cup each of whole wheat and all-purpose flour. Gradually add 2½ cups water and mix with a heavy duty mixer or beat with a wooden spoon until well mixed. Mix in proofed yeast and wheat germ or bran. Gradually stir in enough of the remaining flour to make a soft dough; you may not need to use all of it. Mix in nuts and herbs. Knead with mixer's dough hook or transfer to a lightly floured board and knead by hand for 10 minutes. Place kneaded dough in a lightly oiled bowl, cover with plastic wrap and let rise until doubled in size, about 1½ hours.

Punch down dough and transfer to a lightly floured board. Divide dough into 4 equal pieces and shape each piece into a long slender loaf. Place loaves several inches apart on 2 oiled baking sheets. Or, shape each dough piece into a round ball and place each in an oiled 9-inch pie pan. Cover and let rise until doubled in size, about 45 to 50 minutes.

Heat oven to 375°. Bake bread for 30 to 35 minutes, or until golden brown; loaves should sound hollow when thumped. Cool on a rack. Slip extra loaves into locking plastic bags and freeze until ready to serve.

ITALIAN COUNTRY HERB BREAD

Makes 2 loaves

Using a starter (also called a sponge or biga), this bread develops a depth of flavor during its slow rise.

STARTER

1 tsp. active dry yeast
⅓ cup lukewarm water
⅔ cup milk, room temperature
1 tsp. honey
2 cups unbleached all-purpose flour

DOUGH

1 tsp. active dry yeast
2 cups water
1 tbs. salt
3 cups unbleached all-purpose flour
2-2½ cups whole wheat flour
½ cup minced mixed fresh oregano, sage, basil and flat-leaf parsley

For starter, sprinkle yeast over water and milk in a large bowl; stir to dissolve. Add honey and flour and beat until smooth. Cover with plastic wrap and let stand at room temperature for at least 4 hours or overnight. If desired, store in the refrigerator for up to 1 week before using, or freeze for longer storage. After using ½ of the starter, replenish with ½ cup water and 1 cup flour and return to refrigerator for the next use.

For dough, place yeast, water, salt and 1 cup of the all-purpose flour in a bowl and let stand until dissolved and puffy, about 10 minutes. Add ½ of the starter and beat vigorously for 3 minutes with a heavy duty mixer's paddle attachment for 3 minutes, or with a wooden spoon for 5 minutes. Continue to add whole wheat and all-purpose flour, 1 cup at a time, and herbs and beat until dough is smooth and clings together; you may not need to use all of the flour. Transfer to a lightly floured board and knead until smooth, yet still soft. Place in a lightly oiled bowl, cover with plastic wrap and let rise until tripled in size, about 4 hours.

Punch down dough and transfer to a lightly floured board. Divide dough in half and shape each half into a round. Or, form each half into 2 logs about 16 inches long. Place dough on oiled baking sheets, cover and let rise until light and springy, up to 2 hours.

Heat oven to 400°. Bake bread for 30 to 35 minutes, or until golden brown; loaves should sound hollow when thumped. Cool on a rack.

ITALIAN PARMESAN HERB BREAD

This fine-textured brioche-style loaf is laced with herbs and cheese for eye-catching appeal and delicious flavor.

1 pkg. active dry yeast
1 cup lukewarm water
2 tbs. sugar
1 tsp. salt
3½ cups unbleached all-purpose flour
4 eggs
½ cup unsalted butter, room temperature
¾ cup (3 oz.) freshly grated Parmesan cheese
1 cup (4 oz.) shredded fontina, Gruyère or
   Jarlsberg cheese
½ cup roughly minced fresh basil or mixed
   fresh sage and oregano

In a large bowl, sprinkle yeast into water and let stand until dissolved and puffy, about 10 minutes. Add sugar, salt and 1 cup of the flour; beat well with a heavy duty mixer or wooden spoon. Add 3 of the eggs, one at a time, beating until smooth. Beat in butter. Gradually stir in enough remaining flour to make a soft dough; you may not need to use all of it. Knead with mixer's dough hook for about 2 to 3 minutes; Or, transfer dough to a lightly floured board and knead by hand for about 10 minutes, until smooth and satiny. Place kneaded dough in an oiled bowl. Butter the top of dough lightly and cover with plastic wrap. Let rise in a warm place until doubled in size, about 1½ to 2 hours.

Punch down dough and transfer to a lightly floured board. Knead dough lightly and divide in half. Roll out each piece into a rectangle about 10 x 16 inches. Beat remaining egg and blend in cheeses and herbs. Spread cheese filling over dough. Roll up dough firmly, jelly roll-fashion, from a wide side. Place rolls on 2 oiled baking sheets. With scissors, snip each loaf straight down at 1¼-inch intervals, cutting almost through the dough. Pull and twist each segment so that it lays flat to reveal a pinwheel of filling, and place segments on opposite sides. Cover and let rise in a warm place until doubled in size, about 45 to 50 minutes.

Heat oven to 350°. Bake bread for 30 to 40 minutes, or until golden brown; loaves should sound hollow when thumped. Cool on a rack.

FOCACCIA SUNFLOWER

The unique way of shaping this loaf like a sunflower results in easy-to-pull-apart slices at serving time. Accompany with **Basil Pesto**, *page 21, or* **Sun-Dried Tomato and Roasted Garlic Pesto**, *page 23, for a savory appetizer.*

1 pkg. active dry yeast
¼ cup lukewarm water
pinch sugar or honey
1¼ cups water
2 tbs. olive oil plus more for brushing
3 cups unbleached all-purpose flour
1½ tsp. salt
¼ cup cornmeal or wheat bran
2-3 tbs. chopped fresh rosemary

In a large bowl, sprinkle yeast into ¼ cup water, add sugar and let stand until dissolved and puffy, about 10 minutes. Stir in 1¼ cups water and 2 tbs. oil. Add 1 cup of the flour and salt and mix with a heavy duty mixer or wooden spoon until smooth. Stir in cornmeal and remaining flour, ½ cup at a time, until dough comes together. Knead with a heavy duty mixer's dough hook or by hand for about 8 to 10 minutes. Place kneaded dough in a lightly oiled bowl, cover with plastic wrap and let rise until doubled in size, about 1½ hours.

Punch down dough, transfer to a lightly floured board and knead lightly. Roll out dough into a 14-inch round and place on a pizza pan. With a glass turned upside down, make a 3-inch round indentation in the center. With a pastry scraper or knife, divide the outer circle into quarters; then cut each quarter into halves, making eighths, and each eighth into halves to make 16 slices. Pick up the end of each strip, twist and fold over to lay flat. Cover and let rise until doubled in size, about 45 to 50 minutes.

Heat oven to 425°. Brush dough with olive oil and sprinkle with rosemary. Bake for 20 to 25 minutes or until golden brown. Cool on a rack. Pull pieces apart to serve.

LAVENDER FOCACCIA WITH GRAPES

Makes 1 large rectangular, or two 9-inch round loaves

A crusty focaccia, aromatic with lavender and bursting with the sweetness of grapes, makes a chewy and conversational appetizer. Or, let it accompany a salad luncheon.

1 pkg. active dry yeast
¼ cup lukewarm water
1¼ cups water
1½ tbs. olive oil
3 cups unbleached all-purpose flour
3 tbs. sugar
3 tbs. fresh lavender blossoms or minced
   fresh lemon balm
1½ tsp. salt
olive oil for brushing
2 cups seedless grapes

In a large bowl, sprinkle yeast into ¼ cup water and let stand until dissolved and puffy, about 10 minutes. Stir in remaining water and oil. Add 1 cup of the flour, sugar, lavender and salt and mix with a heavy duty mixer or wooden spoon until smooth. Stir in remaining flour, ½ cup at a time, until dough comes together. Knead with a heavy duty mixer's dough hook or transfer to a lightly floured board and knead by hand for about 8 to 10 minutes. Place dough in a lightly oiled bowl, cover with plastic wrap and let rise until doubled in size, about 1½ hours.

Punch down dough, transfer to a lightly floured board and knead lightly. Roll out dough to fit a 10-x-15-inch baking sheet. Or, divide dough in half and shape into 9-inch rounds. Place dough on oiled baking sheet or pie pans. With fingers, make several depressions about 1 inch apart. Brush dough with olive oil. Push grapes into depressions. Cover dough and let rise until doubled in size, about 45 to 50 minutes.

Heat oven to 425°. Bake bread for 15 to 20 minutes, or until golden brown; loaf should sound hollow when thumped.

HERB-GLAZED EGG BREAD

A medley of minced fresh herbs lends superb flavor to warm bread.

⅓ cup fruity extra virgin olive oil
3 tbs. dry white wine
2 tbs. lemon juice
2 cloves garlic, minced
2 green onions, minced
2 tbs. minced fresh flat-leaf parsley
   or chervil
1 tbs. minced fresh marjoram, lemon
   thyme, tarragon or basil
1 tbs. minced fresh dill, optional
1 loaf egg bread or crusty country-style white bread, cut into 12 slices

Heat oven to 350°. Combine all ingredients, except bread, in a small bowl and stir to blend. Brush mixture on cut sides of bread and reassemble loaf. Wrap with aluminum foil and bake for 10 minutes, or until hot throughout.

SOUPS AND SALADS

MUSTARD TARRAGON SOUP

This zestful soup makes a conversational first course or pass-around starter for guests.

4 shallots, coarsely chopped
1 tsp. olive oil
3 cups chicken stock
1 tbs. minced fresh tarragon
1 tsp. minced fresh thyme or chervil
2 tbs. whole-grain mustard
1 clove garlic, minced
1/4 cup dry white wine

salt and pepper to taste
1 tbs. cornstarch blended with 1 tbs. cold water
1/3 cup heavy cream
toasted baguette slices
grated Romano or dry Monterey Jack cheese

In a large saucepan, sauté shallots in oil over medium-high heat until soft and slightly golden. Add stock, tarragon, thyme, mustard, garlic, wine, salt and pepper and bring to a boil. Reduce heat to low and simmer for 10 minutes. Add cornstarch paste and cook, stirring, until thickened. Cool slightly and puree with a blender or food processor until smooth. Add cream and heat through; do not boil. Serve in mugs informally, or in small bowls for a first course. Accompany with toasted baguette slices topped with cheese and broiled until melted and lightly browned.

PROVENÇAL VEGETABLE SOUP

The first-of-the-season young fresh vegetables are excellent in this aromatic soup. Accompany with crusty French bread and a fruit and cheese board.

1 qt. chicken stock
4 small new potatoes, diced
2 small carrots, sliced
1/3 lb. green beans or Italian beans, cut into 1-inch lengths
1 small yellow crookneck squash, thinly sliced

1 small zucchini, thinly sliced
1 leek, white part only, sliced
1/3 cup shelled fresh peas
2 cloves garlic, minced
2 tomatoes, peeled and chopped
2 tbs. minced fresh flat-leaf parsley
3 tbs. minced fresh basil

Bring stock to a boil in a large saucepan. Add potatoes and carrots, reduce heat to low and simmer for 8 minutes. Add beans, squash, zucchini and leek and simmer for 5 minutes. Add peas, garlic, tomatoes and parsley and heat through. Ladle into soup bowls. Sprinkle with basil.

PINTO BEAN AND BARLEY SOUP

Servings: 8-10

Orange peel punctuates this hearty Northern Italian full-meal soup. Crusty whole-grain bread, a wedge of Asiago or dry jack cheese, a bottle of Zinfandel or Barbera wine and a bowl of fresh fruit can round out the meal.

¾ cup pearl barley
water
1 tbs. olive oil
2 medium onions, chopped
3 large carrots, chopped
2 stalks fennel or celery, chopped
1 cup dried pinto or cranberry beans, soaked overnight, drained
1 cup dry red wine

8 cups chicken stock
4 cloves garlic, minced
3 bay leaves
6 strips orange peel (zest), thinly slivered
2 yams or sweet potatoes, peeled and cubed
salt and freshly ground pepper to taste
⅓ cup *Basil Pesto*, page 21, or *Oregano Pesto*, page 22, plus more to pass

Soak barley in water to cover for 1 hour; drain. In a soup pot, heat oil over medium heat and sauté onions, carrots and fennel for 3 to 4 minutes, or until softened. Add beans and wine and bring to a boil; boil for 2 to 3 minutes. Add stock, garlic, bay leaves and orange peel. Reduce heat to low, cover and simmer for 1 hour. Add soaked barley and yams and simmer for 30 minutes, until barley, yams and beans are tender. Season with salt and pepper. Stir in ⅓ cup pesto and ladle into bowls. Pass additional pesto.

JAMAICAN CARROT SOUP

This is a favorite soup for all seasons: serve it warm in winter and chilled in summer. Lemon balm lends a special lift to the finish. If using canned chicken stock, select the low-salt variety.

1 large onion, chopped
4 large carrots, cut into 1-inch chunks
1/8 tsp. nutmeg
2 tsp. minced fresh ginger
3 cloves garlic, chopped
3 cups water or chicken stock
dash hot pepper sauce

salt and pepper to taste
3 tbs. crunchy peanut butter
plain yogurt for garnish
2 tbs. minced fresh lemon balm,
    marjoram or flat-leaf parsley
    for garnish

Place onion, carrots, nutmeg, ginger, garlic, water and hot pepper sauce in a large saucepan and bring to a boil. Reduce heat to low, cover and simmer until vegetables are very tender, about 20 minutes. Cool soup slightly and puree with a blender or food processor with salt, pepper and peanut butter. Serve soup warm or chilled, garnished with a dollop of yogurt and a shower of herbs.

LEEK AND SUNCHOKE SOUP

The duo of nutty sunchokes and caramelized leeks makes an unbeatable combination in this zestful soup. If you're counting calories, omit the cream and substitute yogurt. When sunchokes are out of season, sweet potatoes are a delicious stand-in.

1 lb. sunchokes (Jerusalem artichokes)
juice of ½ lemon
2 tsp. olive oil
1 large bunch leeks, white part only, chopped
1 medium onion, chopped
1 inner stalk celery with leaves, chopped
1 clove garlic, minced

4 cups chicken stock, or 4 chicken bouillon cubes and 4 cups water
⅓ cup heavy cream or plain yogurt
2 tsp. minced fresh tarragon
2 tsp. minced fresh chives
salt and pepper to taste
plain yogurt and chopped fresh chives for garnish

Wash, peel and slice sunchokes and drop into a bowl of cold water with lemon juice as you work. In a large saucepan, heat olive oil over medium-high heat and sauté leeks, onion and celery for about 8 to 10 minutes, or until soft. Add drained sunchokes and garlic and sauté for a few minutes. Add stock and bring to a boil. Reduce heat to low, cover and simmer for 20 to 30 minutes, or until sunchokes are tender. Cool slightly. Puree soup with a blender or food processor with cream, tarragon, chives, salt and pepper. Heat through and ladle into soup bowls. Garnish with a dollop of yogurt and sprinkle with chives.

AVGOLEMONO AND SORREL SOUP

This favorite Greek egg and lemon soup gets a tangy lift from sorrel. It is appealing served in small sippable cups or bowls as a pass-around starter to a patio guest dinner.

3/4 cup chopped fresh sorrel
2 leeks, white part only, chopped
1 tbs. unsalted butter or olive oil
3 cups chicken stock, preferably homemade
1 1/2 tbs. cornstarch mixed with 1 1/2 tbs. cold water
3 eggs
1/4 cup lemon juice
lemon slices for garnish
chopped fresh chives for garnish

In a saucepan, sauté sorrel and leeks in butter over medium heat until leeks are glazed and sorrel changes color, about 5 minutes. Add stock and bring to a boil. Stir in cornstarch paste and cook for 2 minutes. In a heatproof bowl, whisk together eggs and lemon juice. Pour 1/2 of the stock mixture into egg mixture, whisking constantly. Return mixture to saucepan and cook over very low heat, stirring constantly, until thickened. Do not boil or soup will curdle. Ladle into soup bowls, small tea cups or soufflé dishes and garnish each with a lemon slice and chives.

ROMA TOMATO SOUP

Vine-ripened tomatoes create a succulent sweet soup that is superb hot or cold.

1 medium onion, chopped
2 stalks celery, chopped
1 carrot, grated
2 tbs. olive oil
2 cloves garlic, minced
1 can (6 oz.) tomato paste
6 whole cloves, tied in a small square of cheesecloth
1 qt. chicken stock
12 Roma tomatoes, peeled
salt and pepper to taste
1/4 cup minced fresh basil
plain yogurt or sour cream for garnish
basil sprigs for garnish

In a large saucepan, sauté onion, celery and carrot in oil over medium-high heat until glazed. Add garlic, tomato paste, cloves, chicken stock, tomatoes, salt and pepper and simmer for 15 minutes. Remove cloves. Cool soup slightly and puree with a food processor or blender. Add minced basil and puree slightly. Serve soup hot or chilled, garnished with yogurt and basil sprigs.

HONFLEUR FISH STEW

Honfleur, a town in Normandy, France, is famous for its picturesque bobbing boats and this rustic anise-flavored stew. Fast to prepare, it makes a perfect midweek dinner entrée.

1 tbs. butter or olive oil
1 medium onion, chopped
1 leek, white part only, chopped
2 stalks fennel, chopped
4 cups chicken stock
1 cup dry white wine
2 medium Yukon Gold or white potatoes,
   peeled and cut into 1-inch chunks

1 bay leaf
1/2 tsp. fennel seeds
1 lb. boneless rockfish, red snapper or
   halibut
salt and freshly ground pepper to taste
1/4 cup minced fresh chives, fennel or
   flat-leaf parsley for garnish

Heat butter or oil in a large saucepan over medium heat and sauté onion, leek and fennel until soft. Add chicken stock and wine and bring to a boil. Add potatoes, bay leaf and fennel seeds and bring to a boil. Reduce heat to low, cover and simmer until vegetables are tender, about 20 minutes. Cut fish into small chunks and add to soup. Cover and simmer for about 10 minutes, or until fish separates when tested with a fork. Season with salt and pepper and serve topped with herbs.

PARSLEY SALAD

This zestful salad, a specialty of the Parisian restaurant Arpegé, makes a delightful accompaniment to grilled fish.

2 cups minced fresh flat-leaf parsley, or part chervil
1/4 cup chopped arugula
2 tbs. mixed chopped fresh chives, dill, tarragon and thyme
2 tbs. extra virgin olive oil
1 tsp. lemon juice
salt and pepper to taste

In a bowl, place herbs and arugula. Add oil, lemon juice, salt and pepper and mix lightly.

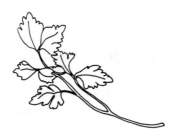

DILL-MARINATED CUCUMBERS

This classic Scandinavian salad is delightful with seafood or grilled fish.

1 long English cucumber, or 3 regular cucumbers, peeled and thinly sliced
salt
water
½ cup white wine vinegar
2 tbs. water
¼ cup sugar
2 tbs. minced fresh dill
¼ tsp. white pepper
3 tbs. minced fresh flat-leaf parsley

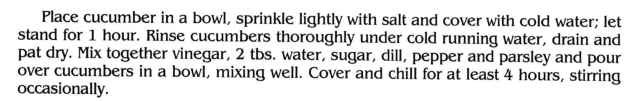

Place cucumber in a bowl, sprinkle lightly with salt and cover with cold water; let stand for 1 hour. Rinse cucumbers thoroughly under cold running water, drain and pat dry. Mix together vinegar, 2 tbs. water, sugar, dill, pepper and parsley and pour over cucumbers in a bowl, mixing well. Cover and chill for at least 4 hours, stirring occasionally.

LAYERED GAZPACHO SALAD

A spring-topped, wide-mouthed canning jar is an ideal container for holding this colorful salad as it marinates and totes to a picnic. Lemon cucumbers can be found in specialty markets or at farmers markets in the summertime.

2 large tomatoes, peeled and thinly sliced
2 lemon cucumbers, or 1 small cucumber, peeled and thinly sliced
1 red or yellow bell pepper, cut into matchstick strips
1/4 lb. mushrooms, sliced
1 red onion, sliced
1 tbs. minced fresh chives
1 tbs. minced fresh basil
salt and freshly ground pepper to taste
8 oil-cured black olives, pitted
Garlic Basil Vinaigrette, follows
basil sprigs for garnish

In a large wide-mouthed jar or bowl, alternate layers of tomatoes, cucumbers, pepper strips, mushrooms, onion slices and minced herbs. Sprinkle each layer with salt and pepper and top with olives. Add *Garlic Basil Vinaigrette*. Cover and chill for at least 1 hour. Garnish with basil sprigs.

GARLIC BASIL VINAIGRETTE

Makes about ½ cup

¼ cup olive oil
1½ tbs. tarragon-flavored white wine vinegar
1½ tbs. dry white wine
1 tbs. chopped fresh basil
1 clove garlic, minced
salt and pepper to taste

Mix all ingredients until well blended.

FRUIT AND FETA SALAD

Servings: 4

The sweet, tangy accent of lemon grass and lemon balm links fruit, cheese and greens in this refreshing salad plate.

4 cups mixed greens: butter lettuce, red
   oakleaf lettuce, arugula and/or mache
Lemon Balm Dressing, follows
1 cup strawberries, hulled and halved
1 cup seedless grapes

3 oz. feta cheese, diced
3 tbs. toasted chopped pistachio nuts
   or pecans
lemon balm sprigs for garnish

Place greens in a bowl, add dressing and toss to coat thoroughly. Add berries, grapes and cheese and mix lightly. Spoon onto salad plates, sprinkle with nuts and garnish with lemon balm sprigs.

Makes about 1/3 cup

LEMON BALM DRESSING

2 tbs. canola oil
2 tbs. olive oil
1 tsp. Dijon mustard
2 tbs. raspberry vinegar
1 tbs. dry white wine
1 tsp. cassis (black currant) syrup

1 shallot, chopped
1 tsp. minced fresh lemon grass or
   lemon peel (zest)
2 tsp. minced fresh lemon balm
salt and freshly ground pepper to taste

In a small jar, shake together dressing ingredients until blended.

FENNEL- AND FISH-STUFFED TOMATOES

Servings: 4

A canopied cafe on the sandy beach of Skiathos, Greece, offers big plump tomatoes stuffed with this seafood medley among the lunch-time offerings.

¾ lb. cold poached snapper, halibut,
   sole or turbot fillets
1 bulb fennel, trimmed and diced
¼ cup olive oil
2 tbs. fresh lemon juice
1 tbs. white wine vinegar
salt and freshly ground pepper to taste
2 green onions, chopped

4 leaves fresh mint, chopped
3 tbs. minced fresh flat-leaf parsley
2 tbs. minced fresh dill or fennel
2 tbs. pine nuts
4 medium tomatoes
salad greens
12 kalamata olives for garnish

Flake fish coarsely into a medium bowl and add diced fennel. Combine oil, lemon juice, vinegar, salt, pepper, onions, herbs and pine nuts; add to fish, mixing lightly. Core tomatoes, scoop out tomato pulp and reserve pulp for another use. Spoon fish salad into tomato shells and chill until serving time. Serve on plates lined with greens and garnish with olives.

ASPARAGUS AND SHRIMP SALAD

For an easy, fast dinner, savor fresh asparagus with shrimp in a cool salad.

½ lb. fresh asparagus, ends trimmed
salad greens
2 large tomatoes, cored
½ lb. cooked small shrimp

1 stalk celery, chopped
2 tbs. minced fresh chives
Tarragon Vinaigrette, follows

Steam asparagus over barely simmering water for 4 to 5 minutes, or until tender-crisp; cool. Arrange greens on large plates. Cut tomatoes into sixths, cutting not quite through, and place each on a pile of greens. Toss shrimp with celery and chives and spoon into the center of tomatoes. Arrange asparagus alongside and drizzle with *Tarragon Vinaigrette*.

TARRAGON VINAIGRETTE

Makes about ⅓ cup

2 tbs. canola or olive oil
2 tbs. white wine vinegar
1 tbs. lemon juice
2 tsp. minced fresh tarragon

1 tsp. Dijon mustard
1 shallot, minced, or 1 tbs. minced red
   onion

In a small jar, shake together vinaigrette ingredients until blended.

GREEN BEAN, MUSHROOM AND SEAFOOD SALAD

A choice of seafood can embellish this fresh-tasting full-meal salad. Commence the meal with a cool cucumber soup and finish off with cantaloupe or Crenshaw melon wedges à la mode.

½ lb. green beans, cut in half lengthwise
¼ lb. white mushrooms, sliced
1 shallot, chopped
¼ cup diced jicama, optional
2 tbs. olive oil
2 tbs. white wine vinegar
1 tsp. minced fresh tarragon

1 tsp. Dijon mustard
salt and pepper to taste
salad greens
½ lb. cooked scallops, mussels or
   medium shrimp
2 tbs. minced fresh flat-leaf parsley,
   chervil or chives

Cook beans in boiling salted water for 5 to 7 minutes, or until tender-crisp. Drain and rinse under cold running water; drain again. Place beans in a bowl and add mushrooms, shallot and jicama, if using. Mix together oil, vinegar, tarragon, mustard, salt and pepper. Pour dressing over vegetables and mix lightly. Arrange greens on plates and spoon vegetable medley on top. Ring with seafood. Sprinkle with herbs.

WHEAT BERRY HERB-BALSAMIC SALAD

This healthful grain makes a delightful cool salad to keep on hand for a quick lunch or dinner accompaniment.

1⅓ cups wheat berries
4 cups water
salt to taste
3 tbs. balsamic or red wine vinegar
1 tbs. extra virgin olive oil
peel (zest) of 1 orange, slivered
salt and pepper to taste

1 medium red onion, finely chopped
2 cloves garlic, minced
8 oil-packed sun-dried tomatoes,
  snipped, optional
¼ cup mixed minced fresh chives,
  flat-leaf parsley and oregano or
  marjoram

Place wheat berries in a large skillet and heat over medium heat, stirring constantly, until berries exude a popping sound and are lightly toasted. Transfer to a saucepan and add water and salt. Bring to a boil. Reduce heat to low, cover and simmer until tender-crunchy, about 1 hour; drain off any extra liquid. Combine vinegar, oil, orange peel, salt, pepper, onion, garlic and tomatoes; pour over wheat berries and mix lightly. Chill. Sprinkle with herbs at serving time.

LEMON GRASS TABBOULEH WITH SHRIMP

For an informal appetizer when everyone scoops their own, this take on a Middle Eastern wheat salad is a hit at an outdoor gathering. Or, serve it on small plates for a first course or salad. Lemon grass and cilantro lend an intriguing flavor.

1½ cups boiling water
1 cup bulgur wheat
1¼ cups cilantro sprigs
¼ cup fresh mint leaves, packed
2 tbs. minced fresh lemon grass or
   lemon balm
3 cloves garlic, minced

⅓ cup pistachio nuts or pine nuts
3 tbs. olive oil
¼ cup lemon juice
½ tsp. salt
½ tsp. ground allspice
¾ lb. cooked small shrimp
romaine lettuce leaves

Pour water over bulgur in a bowl. Cover and let stand for 15 minutes; cool to room temperature. With a blender or food processor, process cilantro, mint, lemon grass, garlic, nuts, oil, lemon juice, salt and allspice until finely minced. Add to bulgur and mix lightly with a fork to separate grains. Cover and chill for 2 hours.

At serving time, mound tabbouleh on a platter. Ring with shrimp and romaine leaves. Encourage guests to use romaine leaves as scoopers.

PASTA SALAD WITH TOMATOES AND LEEKS

Servings: 4

Serve this pasta salad tepid or chilled for a summer supper, accompanied by chilled steamed asparagus spears or artichokes.

1 leek, white part only, chopped
3 tbs. olive oil
8 oz. dried small shell pasta
3 tbs. lemon juice
1 shallot or green onion, finely chopped
2 tsp. minced fresh basil or oregano
salt and freshly ground pepper to taste

¼ cup minced fresh flat-leaf parsley
½ cup oil-packed sun-dried tomatoes, snipped
½ cup (2 oz.) crumbled goat cheese or feta cheese
basil or parsley sprigs for garnish

In a small skillet over medium heat, sauté leek in 1 tsp. of the oil until soft. In a large pot of rapidly boiling salted water, cook pasta until slightly firm to the bite, *al dente*, about 10 minutes. Drain pasta, leaving a little water clinging to it and cool for a few minutes.

In a large bowl, stir together remaining oil, lemon juice, shallot, basil, salt and pepper. Add pasta and toss to coat. Stir in leeks, parsley, tomatoes and goat cheese. Serve at room temperature or chilled, garnished with basil or parsley sprigs.

SHRIMP AND ROTELLE SALAD

The crunch of fresh corn is delightful in this herb-scented corkscrew salad.

8 oz. dried rotelle or other pasta
2 cloves garlic, minced
2 tsp. grated fresh lemon peel (zest)
2 tbs. fresh lemon juice
1 tbs. white wine vinegar
3 tbs. extra virgin olive oil
6 oz. cooked small shrimp

2 ears white or yellow corn, cooked,
   chilled and cut from the cob
1 small red onion, chopped
1/3 cup minced fresh basil
1/4 cup minced fresh flat-leaf parsley
3/4 cup cherry tomatoes
basil or parsley sprigs for garnish

In a large pot of rapidly boiling salted water, cook pasta until slightly firm to the bite, *al dente*, about 8 to 10 minutes. Drain pasta, leaving a little water clinging to it; cool. In a large bowl, stir together garlic, lemon peel, lemon juice, vinegar and oil, and toss with pasta, shrimp, corn, onion, basil, parsley and tomatoes. Chill for 1 hour. Garnish with a few parsley or basil sprigs.

ANGEL HAIR PASTA SALAD WITH SMOKED TROUT AND DILL

Excellent smoked fish is available in delicatessens and markets, ready to pair with dill in an enticing summer salad for a luncheon or weekend brunch. Look for lemon cucumbers with the specialty produce.

8 oz. dried angel hair pasta
2 tbs. olive oil
¼ cup light-style sour cream
¼ cup plain yogurt
1 tbs. minced fresh dill or fennel
1 tbs. minced fresh chives
3 cups mixed gourmet greens, or
    flat-leaf parsley and arugula sprigs

8 oz. smoked trout, flaked, or smoked
    salmon, cut into strips
2 cups halved cherry tomatoes
2 small lemon cucumbers, or 1 small
    cucumber, peeled and sliced
2 hard-cooked eggs, shredded
dill or fennel sprigs for garnish

Cook pasta in boiling salted water until slightly firm to the bite, *al dente*. Drain and rinse under cold water; drain again. Place pasta in a large bowl and toss with oil. Mix together sour cream, yogurt and herbs and reserve 2 tbs. of the mixture; toss remaining mixture with pasta. Ring serving plates with greens, spoon pasta in the center and top with fish. Ring with tomatoes and overlap cucumber slices. Sprinkle with shredded egg, dollop with reserved dressing and garnish with dill sprigs.

ORZO WITH FETA AND SHRIMP

The tear-shaped specialty pasta called orzo brings a toothsome texture to this cold pasta salad. It is a fine choice to carry on a picnic or to a potluck.

8 oz. dried orzo
1/4 cup olive oil
1 1/2 tbs. lemon juice
1 shallot or green onion, finely chopped
2 tbs. minced fresh dill
salt and pepper to taste
3/4 cup (3 oz.) crumbled feta cheese

1/4 cup minced fresh flat-leaf parsley or basil
1/2 cup oil-packed sun-dried tomatoes, snipped
6 oz. cooked small shrimp
parsley or basil leaves for garnish

In a large pot of rapidly boiling salted water, cook orzo until slightly firm to the bite, *al dente*, about 10 to 12 minutes. Drain pasta, leaving a little water clinging to it and cool for a few minutes.

In a large bowl, stir together oil, lemon juice, shallot, dill, salt and pepper. Add pasta and toss to coat. Stir in feta, parsley or basil, tomatoes and shrimp; chill. At serving time, garnish with parsley or basil leaves.

TUNA AND ARTICHOKE PASTA SALAD

This summer salad can rely on pantry staples for the basic ingredients.

8 oz. dried tubular pasta, such as penne
 or large elbow macaroni
1 tbs. minced fresh ginger
2 cloves garlic, minced
2 tsp. grated fresh lemon peel (zest)
3 tbs. fresh lemon juice
3 tbs. extra virgin olive oil
1 can (6 oz.) albacore tuna, drained and
 flaked

1 can (8½ oz.) artichoke hearts, drained
 and quartered, or 1½ cups frozen
 petite peas, thawed
3 green onions, chopped
⅓ cup minced fresh basil or flat-leaf
 parsley
¾ cup cherry tomatoes
basil or parsley sprigs for garnish

In a large pot of rapidly boiling salted water, cook pasta until slightly firm to the bite, *al dente*, about 8 to 10 minutes. Drain pasta, leaving a little water clinging to it, and cool for a few minutes. In a large bowl, stir together ginger, garlic, lemon peel, lemon juice and oil, and toss with pasta, tuna, artichokes, onions, basil and tomatoes. Cover and chill for 1 hour. At serving time, garnish with a few basil or parsley sprigs.

CHICKEN AND MANGO SALAD

Servings: 2

Lemon grass and lemon balm make a refreshing counterpoint in this chicken and mango salad.

2 cooked chicken breast halves,
   skinned and boned
Sesame Soy Dressing, follows
butter lettuce or mixed salad greens

1 mango, peeled and sliced, or ½
   cantaloupe, sliced
1 cup hulled and halved strawberries
2 tbs. minced fresh lemon balm

Tear chicken meat into strips, place in a bowl and toss with ½ of the dressing. Arrange lettuce on plates and spoon chicken on top. Ring with mango and berries. Scatter lemon balm over the top and drizzle with remaining dressing.

SESAME SOY DRESSING

Makes about ⅓ cup

2 tbs. safflower oil
1 tbs. soy sauce
1 tbs. sesame oil
1 tbs. lemon juice

2 tsp. honey
½ tsp. minced fresh lemon grass or
   grated fresh lemon peel (zest)
dash hot pepper sauce, optional

Stir all ingredients together until well blended.

VEGETABLES

VINEYARD BRUSSELS SPROUTS

Grapes, pistachios and fresh tarragon bring a festive touch to sprouts.

1 lb. Brussels sprouts
1 tbs. olive oil or butter
1 cup seedless red or green grapes
2 tbs. dry white wine
dash salt and pepper
2 tsp. minced fresh tarragon
3 tbs. pistachio nuts or slivered almonds,
    toasted

In a medium saucepan, cook sprouts in boiling salted water until tender, about 5 to 7 minutes; drain water from pan. Add oil to pan and heat gently, shaking pan to coat sprouts lightly with oil. Add grapes, wine, salt, pepper and tarragon and cook until heated through. Serve sprinkled with nuts.

CABBAGE WEDGES WITH FENNEL

A fast simmer of cabbage wedges in milk with fennel makes a healthy vegetable dish.

½ head green cabbage
¾ cup milk
1 tsp. fennel seeds
1 tbs. minced fresh fennel
salt and pepper to taste

Cut cabbage into 4 wedges, trimming the core. Place cabbage wedges in a saucepan with milk and fennel seeds and bring to a boil. Reduce heat to low, cover and simmer for 4 to 5 minutes, or until cabbage is tender-crisp. With a slotted spoon, transfer cabbage to plates, sprinkle with fresh fennel and season with salt and pepper.

ANISE CARROTS

Tarragon and star anise lend a bright licorice note to this simple vegetable side dish or salad. Star anise is a dark brown pod that contains a seed in each of its eight segments. Available in some supermarkets and Asian markets, it is one of the ingredients in Chinese five-spice powder.

6 medium carrots, sliced thinly on the diagonal
3 tbs. lemon juice
2 tbs. fruity olive oil
1/4 tsp. ground allspice

1 pod star anise
1/8 tsp. five-spice powder
2 green onions, white part only, chopped
1 tbs. minced fresh tarragon
2 tbs. minced fresh flat-leaf parsley

In a saucepan, cook carrots in boiling salted water until tender-crisp, about 6 to 8 minutes; drain. In a bowl, mix together lemon juice, olive oil, allspice, star anise, five spice powder, onions and tarragon. Add carrots, cover and chill. At serving time, remove star anise and garnish with parsley.

CHERVIL CARROTS AND SUGAR SNAPS

Servings: 4

The snapping-crisp goodness of sugar snap peas and sliced carrots is a great accompaniment to almost any entrée.

4 carrots, sliced diagonally
3 green onions, chopped
½ lb. sugar snap peas or snow pea pods
salt and pepper to taste
1 tbs. minced fresh chervil
2 tsp. unsalted butter, softened

Steam carrots over simmering water for 4 minutes; add onions and sugar snaps and steam for 2 minutes, or until vegetables are tender-crisp. Season with salt and pepper and toss with chervil and butter.

GREEN BEANS WITH TARRAGON

Slender green beans are excellent dressed with herbs.

1 lb. Kentucky wonder, Blue Lake or slender French-style green beans
2 shallots or green onions, chopped
1 clove garlic, minced
1 tbs. olive oil
½ cup thin jicama strips, optional
2 tsp. minced fresh tarragon
2 tbs. minced fresh flat-leaf parsley
salt and pepper to taste

Trim ends from beans and slice lengthwise, or leave French-style beans whole. In a saucepan, cook beans in boiling salted water until tender-crisp, about 5 to 7 minutes; drain. In a skillet, sauté shallots and garlic in oil over medium heat until soft. Add beans, jicama, if using, tarragon, parsley, salt and pepper and shake pan to coat well. Serve hot or cold.

DILLY BEANS

Pickled beans, an old-fashioned condiment, make a zestful addition to a buffet or picnic table. Pack the beans upright in a jar or crock for an appealing and handy way to serve them.

2 cups distilled white vinegar
1 cup water
3 tbs. sugar
1 tsp. salt
1 dried hot red chile
3 cloves garlic
3 sprigs dill, or 1 tsp. dried dill weed
1 small onion, sliced
2 lb. small slender green beans, trimmed

In a medium saucepan, combine vinegar, water, sugar, salt, chile, garlic and dill. Bring to a boil and add onion and beans. Reduce heat to low, cover and simmer for 5 to 8 minutes, or until beans are tender-crisp. Cool and chill overnight to blend flavors. Keeps refrigerated for up to 5 days.

SHALLOTS AND MUSHROOMS BALSAMIC

This hot first course or accompaniment flaunts wine-glazed shallots and plump button mushrooms for a pleasing duo accented with herbs.

2 tbs. unsalted butter
1/4 lb. shallots
2 cloves garlic, minced
1 tbs. chopped fresh ginger, optional
3/4 lb. small button mushrooms, sliced, or shiitake mushrooms, stemmed and sliced
1/4 cup dry sherry
1 tbs. balsamic vinegar
1 tbs. minced fresh tarragon or dill

In a skillet, heat butter over medium heat and sauté shallots, garlic and ginger until soft. Add mushrooms and sauté until glazed. Pour in sherry and vinegar and heat quickly, stirring to coat mushrooms and shallots. Serve in small individual ramekins and top with herbs.

MUSHROOMS À LA GRECQUE

Servings: 6 side dish, or 16 appetizer

Greek-style marinated mushrooms in an herb bath create a zesty dish for an appetizer occasion or an accompaniment to dinner. They also tote with ease to a picnic or potluck. Green and gold zucchini offer a colorful substitute for the mushrooms.

1 lb. white mushrooms
½ cup homemade or low-salt chicken
   stock
1 tbs. olive oil
1½ tbs. lemon juice
1½ tbs. white wine vinegar

1 clove garlic, slivered
4 black peppercorns
¼ tsp. fennel seeds
salt and freshly ground pepper to taste
2 tsp. minced fresh tarragon
3 tbs. minced fresh flat-leaf parsley

Wash mushrooms and pat dry. In a large saucepan, combine chicken stock, oil, lemon juice, vinegar, garlic, peppercorns, fennel seeds, salt and pepper and bring to a boil. Add mushrooms and simmer for 3 to 4 minutes. Remove mushrooms with a slotted spoon and place in a bowl. Boil juices until reduced to a thick sauce. Pour thickened juices over mushrooms, stir in tarragon, cover and chill. Sprinkle with parsley at serving time.

VARIATION: ZUCCHINI À LA GRECQUE

Substitute green and gold zucchini, sliced into ¼-inch rounds, for mushrooms. Substitute 2 tbs. minced fresh basil or oregano for tarragon.

BUTTERNUT SQUASH WITH SAGE

Slow cooking brings out the butternut's natural sugars and fresh sage adds an aromatic accent.

2 tbs. olive oil
1½ lb. butternut squash, peeled, seeded and cut into ¾-inch chunks
2 cloves garlic, minced
1 shallot, minced
salt and freshly ground pepper to taste
1 tbs. minced fresh sage
1 tbs. minced fresh flat-leaf parsley

Heat oil in a large nonstick skillet. Add squash, garlic and shallot and sauté slowly over low heat for about 20 to 25 minutes, or until squash is golden brown and tender. Season with salt and pepper and sprinkle with sage and parsley.

VARIATION: GOLDEN POTATOES WITH SAGE

Substitute Yukon Gold potatoes for butternut squash.

JACKET POTATOES WITH TOPPINGS

In England, popular pub fare are "jacket potatoes," actually baked potatoes that are split and filled with shredded cheddar cheese, baked beans, chopped ham, scrambled eggs or deviled egg salad. Pesto provides an update to the condiment list for a repast of ultimate comfort food.

4 medium-large baking potatoes, such as russet or Yukon Gold
olive oil
Basil Pesto, page 21, *Oregano Pesto*, page 22, or *Sun-Dried Tomato and Roasted Garlic Pesto*, page 23
yogurt or sour cream

chopped green onions or sweet red onions
sliced mushrooms
alfalfa sprouts or diced avocado
crumbled Gorgonzola, feta or goat cheese, or shredded Jarlsberg cheese

Heat oven to 425°. Scrub even-sized, shapely potatoes. Dry potatoes, prick with a fork in several places and rub lightly with oil. Bake for 45 to 50 minutes, or until cooked through. Remove potatoes from oven and slash a cross in the top of each; push up potato insides. Place each potato on a dinner plate. Use individual bowls to hold pesto, yogurt, onions, mushrooms, sprouts and cheese. Pass toppings to spoon over potatoes.

SHREDDED VEGETABLE PANCAKES

A colorful medley of shredded vegetables studs these little pancakes for novel finger food. Or, let them serve as a light entrée with a fruit garnish of seedless grapes and sliced melon.

2 tbs. olive oil
2 green onions, chopped
2 cups shredded carrots, zucchini,
   yellow crookneck squash or
   mushrooms, or a combination

1 egg
½ cup light-style sour cream
3 tbs. cornstarch
1 tbs. minced fresh basil or oregano
salt and freshly ground pepper to taste

In a large skillet, heat 1 tsp. of the oil over medium heat and sauté onions until glazed. Add vegetables and sauté for 1 to 2 minutes, or until tender-crisp, stirring constantly. Remove from heat and cool slightly. Beat egg in a bowl and stir in sour cream, cornstarch, basil, salt, pepper and sautéed vegetables. Heat 1 tsp. of the oil over medium-high heat in skillet and spoon in batter in 1¾-inch rounds. Cook until lightly browned on one side. Turn and lightly brown the opposite side. Repeat with remaining oil and batter.

ARTICHOKE FLOWERS MEXICALI

Spicy Mexican seasonings — cilantro, cumin, oregano, garlic and red pepper — flatter cold boiled artichokes served as a flower with their leaves resembling petals. To savor, dip the leaves into the vinaigrette centering the artichoke.

4 large artichokes
1/4 cup lemon juice
2 tsp. olive oil
2 tbs. sesame oil
2 tbs. white wine vinegar
1 tbs. extra virgin olive oil
1 tbs. lemon juice
1 tbs. minced fresh cilantro
1 shallot or green onion, with 1/2 of the green
    top, minced
1/8 tsp. ground cumin
dash red pepper flakes
1 clove garlic, minced
1 tsp. chopped fresh oregano

With a sharp knife, cut off artichoke stems to make a flat base. Pull off outer leaves and, with scissors, cut thorns from remaining leaves. Cook artichokes in a large pot of boiling salted water with ¼ cup lemon juice and 2 tsp. olive oil, allowing about 40 to 45 minutes for large artichokes. Drain and chill.

Mix together sesame oil, vinegar, 1 tbs. olive oil, 1 tbs. lemon juice, cilantro, shallot, cumin, red pepper flakes, garlic and oregano. With a spoon, scoop out the fuzzy centers or "chokes" of artichokes; discard chokes and place artichokes on a platter. Spoon dressing into centers of artichokes.

VARIATION: ARTICHOKES WITH SHRIMP, YOGURT AND HERBS

3 tbs. plain yogurt
3 tbs. light-style sour cream
1 tsp. fresh lemon juice
½ tsp. Dijon mustard

2 tbs. minced fresh flat-leaf parsley
1 tbs. minced fresh chives, dill or green onion tops
½ lb. cooked small shrimp or crabmeat

Blend together yogurt, sour cream, lemon juice, mustard, parsley and chives. Spoon dressing into centers of artichokes and top with shrimp.

SAGE POLENTA WITH TOMATOES AND OLIVES

With the peppery bite of arugula, the sweet flavor of dried tomatoes and the aromatic quality of sage, this polenta casserole explodes with flavors.

1 cup polenta or yellow cornmeal
3 cups chicken stock
salt and pepper to taste
3 tbs. minced fresh sage
1/4 cup oil-packed sun-dried tomatoes
1/4 cup pitted black olives

3/4 cup (3 oz.) shredded fontina or
    Jarlsberg cheese
1/4 cup (1 oz.) shredded Romano or
    Parmesan cheese
1/3 cup chopped arugula

Heat oven to 300°. Stir polenta into 1 cup of the stock and let stand for 10 minutes. In a deep saucepan, bring remaining stock to a boil and mix in soaked polenta, whisking constantly. Bring to a second boil, reduce heat to low and simmer until thickened, about 15 to 20 minutes, stirring occasionally. Season with salt and pepper and stir in 2 tbs. of the sage. Transfer to an oiled 9-inch pie pan. Scatter tomatoes, olives and cheeses over polenta. Bake for 15 minutes or until heated through. Sprinkle with arugula and remaining sage and cut into wedges.

POLENTA WITH MUSHROOMS AND HERBS

This savory side dish makes a delicious accompaniment to grilled meats or poultry.

1 cup polenta
3½ cups water
2 chicken bouillon cubes
salt and freshly ground pepper to taste
3 tbs. olive oil
½ lb. white or brown mushrooms, sliced

2 cloves garlic, minced
½ cup (2 oz.) shredded Gruyère or
    Jarlsberg cheese
¼ cup mixed minced fresh chives, flat-
    leaf parsley and tarragon

Soak polenta in 1½ cups of the water for 10 minutes. In a deep saucepan, bring remaining 2 cups water to a boil with bouillon cubes and mix in soaked polenta, whisking constantly. Bring to a second boil, reduce heat to low and simmer until thickened, about 15 minutes, stirring occasionally. Season with salt and pepper and stir in 1 tbs. of the oil. Transfer to an oiled 9-inch pie pan. Cool, if making ahead of time, and chill.

Heat oven to 300°. In a large skillet over medium-high heat, sauté mushrooms and garlic in remaining oil until softened and spoon over polenta. Top with cheese. Bake for 15 minutes (25 minutes, if refrigerated) or until heated through. Sprinkle with herbs.

PIZZAS, PASTAS AND EGG DISHES

TORTILLA FLATS

Flour tortillas form a neat base for individual pizzas. Vary the toppings to suit your whim.

1 tbs. olive oil
3 green onions, chopped
1 small zucchini, thinly sliced
1/4 lb. white mushrooms, sliced
1 clove garlic, minced
6 slices salami, or 3 oz. prosciutto, slivered, optional
6 oil-packed sun-dried tomatoes, diced

two 8-inch flour tortillas
3 tbs. tomato paste or spaghetti sauce
1/2 cup (2 oz.) shredded Monterey Jack cheese
2 tbs. grated Romano cheese
2 tbs. minced fresh basil, or 2 tsp. minced fresh oregano

Heat oven to 400°. In a large skillet, heat oil over medium-high heat and sauté onions, zucchini, mushrooms and garlic until softened, about 2 minutes. Add salami, if using, and tomatoes and set aside. Place tortillas on a baking sheet and spread each with tomato paste. Divide vegetable mixture evenly over tortillas and sprinkle with cheeses. Bake for 6 to 8 minutes, or until cheese is melted and tortilla edges are lightly browned. Sprinkle with basil or oregano.

ARMENIAN PIZZA CARTWHEELS

Servings: 2

In this cross-cultural blending of global fare, plate-sized flour tortillas take on a spicy meat and cheese topping for neat individual entrées.

2 tsp. olive oil
1 small sweet onion, thinly sliced, or 4
   green onions, chopped
1 clove garlic, minced
½ lb. ground turkey, lamb or lean beef
½ tsp. cinnamon
½ tsp. ground allspice
2 tbs. chopped fresh flat-leaf parsley
salt and freshly ground pepper to taste

2 tbs. pine nuts or pistachio nuts
2 oz. feta cheese, diced
two 10-inch flour tortillas
¼ cup tomato paste
½ cup (2 oz.) grated Monterey Jack or
   light-style Jarlsberg cheese
1 tbs. chopped fresh basil
1 tbs. chopped fresh oregano

Heat oven to 425°. In a small skillet, heat oil over medium heat and sauté onion and garlic until soft; cool slightly. Place onion mixture in a bowl with meat and lightly mix in cinnamon, allspice, parsley, salt, pepper, nuts and feta cheese. Place tortillas on 2 baking sheets. Spread each tortilla with tomato paste, leaving a ½-inch border. Scatter meat mixture over tomato paste and sprinkle with grated cheese. Bake for 8 to 10 minutes, or until cheese is melted, meat is browned and tortilla edges are lightly browned. Sprinkle with basil and oregano.

SHRIMP AND MUSHROOM TORTILLA PIZZAS

Servings: 2

A large flour tortilla forms a fast cartwheel base for this hot seafood pizza that gets lively pizzazz from a dollop of pesto. It makes an interesting guest lunch or supper entrée with a spinach and avocado salad. Finish off with sliced kiwi fruit and oranges, strawberries or a juicy mango.

1 tbs. olive oil
2 shallots or green onions, white part
  only, chopped
1/4 lb. white or brown mushrooms, sliced
two 8-inch flour tortillas
1/3 cup tomato paste
2 tbs. chopped fresh basil or flat-leaf
  parsley

1/4 lb. cooked small shrimp
8 oil-packed or softened dried sun-
  dried tomatoes, snipped
1/2 cup (2 oz.) shredded Monterey Jack
  or Jarlsberg cheese
Basil Pesto, page 21

Heat oven to 400°. In a small skillet, heat oil over medium heat and sauté shallots until soft; add mushrooms and sauté for 1 minute. Place tortillas on a baking sheet and spread with tomato paste, basil or parsley and sautéed mushrooms. Scatter shrimp, tomatoes and cheese over the top. Bake for 3 to 4 minutes, or until cheese is melted and tortilla edges are lightly browned. Serve on plates and top with pesto.

ROMAN VEGETABLE PIZZAS

Makes four 10-inch pizzas

In Rome, crispy discs of platter-sized pizzas with a dozen different toppings delight the diners in the many casual trattorias. This pizza makes an addictive entrée and it can be varied in impromptu fashion since the dough keeps refrigerated for several days.

DOUGH

¾ cup lukewarm water
1 pkg. active dry yeast
1 tsp. sugar or honey
2 cups unbleached all-purpose flour

¾ tsp. salt
1 egg
1 tbs. olive oil

TOPPING FOR EACH PIZZA

1 tbs. olive oil
1 small red onion, chopped
1 yellow crookneck squash, thinly sliced
1 zucchini, thinly sliced
6 brown mushrooms, thinly sliced
2 Roma tomatoes, sliced

2 oz. mozzarella or Monterey Jack
 cheese, thinly sliced
¼ cup (1 oz.) grated Pecorino Romano
 or Parmesan cheese
3 tbs. torn or minced basil
basil sprigs for garnish

For dough, place water in a large bowl and stir in yeast and sugar. Let stand until dissolved and puffy, about 10 minutes. Mix in 1 cup of the flour, salt, egg and oil. Gradually add remaining flour, mixing with a heavy duty mixer's dough hook or by hand until dough clings together in a ball. Transfer dough to a lightly floured board and knead a few times until dough is no longer sticky. Form dough into a ball and place in a lightly oiled bowl, cover with plastic wrap and let rise until doubled in size, about 1 hour. Gently remove dough from bowl and cut into 4 equal pieces. Use immediately or wrap each piece loosely in plastic wrap and chill for up to 3 days.

Heat oven to 500°, with a pizza stone if desired. Roll out each piece of dough into a 10-inch disk and place on a pizza peel generously sprinkled with cornmeal, or an oiled pizza pan or sheet of aluminum foil. In a large skillet, heat oil over medium heat and sauté onion until soft. Push onion to the side of pan and sauté squashes for 2 minutes; add mushrooms and heat through. Place vegetable mixture on dough with sliced tomatoes; cover with mozzarella. Bake for 6 minutes, or until crust is crisp and browned. Sprinkle with Romano cheese and basil and garnish with basil sprigs.

VARIATION: MUSHROOM AND PROSCIUTTO PIZZAS

Top dough with 2 chopped shallots and ¼ lb. sliced brown mushrooms, sautéed until soft. Top with 2 oz. very thinly sliced prosciutto and 2 oz. thinly sliced mozzarella cheese. Remove from oven and sprinkle with 3 tbs. grated Parmesan cheese and 3 tbs. minced fresh basil or oregano.

PIZZETTE WITH TOMATOES AND HERBS

Once they are shaped, little pizzas take only a few minutes to bake and are convenient to eat out of hand.

DOUGH

1 cup lukewarm water
2 tsp. active dry yeast
1 tsp. honey or sugar
1½ cups unbleached all-purpose flour
¾ tsp. salt
2 tbs. extra virgin olive oil
½ cup whole wheat flour

TOPPING

6 oz. fresh mild light-style goat cheese or feta cheese
2 cups red and gold cherry or small Roma tomatoes, halved
1½ cups (6 oz.) shredded light-style Jarlsberg or Monterey Jack cheese
3 tbs. pine nuts
fresh basil, tarragon or oregano leaves

For dough, place water in a large bowl and stir in yeast and honey. Let stand until dissolved and puffy, about 10 minutes. Mix in 1 cup of the all-purpose flour, salt and oil, mixing until smooth. Gradually add remaining flours, mixing with a heavy duty mixer's dough hook or by hand until dough clings together in a ball. Transfer dough to a lightly floured board and knead until smooth and elastic, about 5 minutes. Form dough into a ball and place in a lightly oiled bowl. Cover with a towel and let dough rise until doubled in size, about 1½ hours.

Punch down dough, divide into quarters, and divide each quarter into 6 balls. On a lightly floured board, roll out each ball into a 4-inch round. Place rounds on oiled baking sheets. Brush dough rounds lightly with olive oil.

Heat oven to 475°. Spread dough rounds with goat cheese and scatter tomatoes over cheese. Top with shredded cheese and nuts. Bake for 5 minutes, or until crust is crisp and browned. Sprinkle with herbs and serve immediately.

CILANTRO SESAME NOODLES

This is a delightful dish to have handy in the refrigerator for a summer luncheon or supper. Strips of grilled or deli-roasted chicken can augment the basic dish.

3 tbs. low-sodium soy sauce
3 tbs. Asian sesame oil
3 tbs. creamy peanut butter
2 tbs. tea or water
2 tbs. rice vinegar
1 tbs. dark brown sugar
2 cloves garlic, minced
2 tsp. minced fresh ginger
8 oz. thin spaghetti or udon noodles

salt and cayenne pepper to taste
3 green onions, with green tops, chopped
1 mango, peeled and sliced, or $1/2$
    cantaloupe, peeled and cut into crescents
$1/2$ cup hulled strawberries or
    blueberries, optional
$1/4$ cup minced fresh cilantro or lemon balm
2 tbs. toasted sesame seeds

In a large bowl, whisk together soy sauce, sesame oil, peanut butter, tea, vinegar, sugar, garlic and ginger; set aside. In a large pot of rapidly boiling salted water, cook pasta according to package directions until slightly firm to the bite, *al dente*; drain and toss with soy sauce mixture, salt, cayenne and onions. Cool to room temperature, cover and chill for 1 hour or longer.

At serving time, arrange noodles on a platter, ring with mango and berries, if using, and sprinkle with cilantro and sesame seeds.

PASTA WITH PESTO PRIMAVERA

Pesto gives an uplift to this wholesome vegetable-laced pasta dish.

1 tbs. olive oil
1 medium zucchini, slivered or thinly
    sliced
1 yellow crookneck squash, slivered or
    thinly sliced
3 green onions, with green tops, chopped
12 sugar snap peas or snow pea pods,
    trimmed
1 tbs. unsalted butter

3 tbs. pine nuts or pistachio nuts
1/3 cup heavy cream
12 cherry tomatoes, halved
1/4 cup *Basil Pesto*, page 21
1/2 lb. fresh fettuccine or tagliarini
1/4 cup freshly grated Romano cheese
2 tbs. slivered fresh basil
basil sprigs for garnish

Heat oil in a large skillet over medium-high heat and sauté squashes, onions and sugar snaps until softened, about 2 minutes; push to the side of pan. Add butter and nuts and sauté until nuts are lightly browned. Add cream, tomatoes and *Basil Pesto* and heat through.

Cook fettuccine in a large pot of rapidly boiling salted water until slightly firm to the bite, *al dente*, about 3 minutes. Drain pasta, leaving a little water clinging to it, and place in a warm bowl. Spoon hot vegetables over pasta in a bowl, mix lightly and spoon onto dinner plates. Sprinkle with cheese and slivered basil and garnish with basil sprigs.

ARTICHOKE FRITTATA SQUARES

Servings: 4 entrée, or 16 appetizer

Marinated artichoke hearts lend a succulent richness to this popular dish, which is ideal both as an entrée or appetizer. It is a good choice for baking ahead and toting to a potluck or picnic.

1 tsp. olive oil
1 medium onion, finely chopped
2 cloves garlic, minced
4 eggs, lightly beaten
2 jars (6 oz. each) marinated artichoke
    hearts, drained and chopped
1/3 cup fine dry breadcrumbs

salt and freshly ground pepper to taste
dash hot pepper sauce
1 cup (4 oz.) shredded sharp cheddar
    cheese
1/4 cup minced fresh flat-leaf parsley
2 tbs. minced fresh oregano or basil

Heat oven to 325°. In a small skillet, heat oil over medium heat and sauté onion and garlic until soft, about 5 minutes. In a bowl, beat eggs and stir in artichoke hearts, sautéed onions, breadcrumbs, salt, pepper, pepper sauce, cheese, parsley and oregano; mix well. Pour into an oiled 9-inch square pan. Bake for 30 minutes, or until eggs are set. Cool frittata in pan and cut into squares.

NOTE: If desired, bake frittata in small nonstick muffin tins, allowing about 20 minutes to cook.

ZUCCHINI FRITTATA

Servings: 6 entrée, or 18 appetizer

When the zucchini bounty is at its height, create this easy one-pan egg dish for an entrée or appetizers.

5 medium zucchini
1 tsp. sea salt
3 tbs. olive oil
2 shallots or green onions, chopped
1 clove garlic, minced
2 Roma tomatoes, peeled, seeded and
    diced

6 eggs
2 tbs. grated Parmesan cheese
freshly ground pepper to taste
1 tbs. minced fresh oregano
1/2 cup (2 oz.) shredded Jarlsberg cheese
2 tbs. minced fresh basil or sorrel
2 tbs. minced fresh flat-leaf parsley

Trim zucchini and cut into very thin strips. Sprinkle with salt and set aside in a colander to drain for 20 minutes; rinse and pat dry. Heat 1 tbs. of the oil in a large skillet over medium heat and sauté zucchini until light golden brown, about 5 to 6 minutes; drain on paper towels. Add 1 tsp. of the oil to skillet and sauté shallots and garlic for 1 minute. Add tomatoes and heat through; transfer to a plate and set aside. Whisk eggs with Parmesan cheese and pepper. Heat remaining oil in skillet, spread zucchini in pan and sprinkle with oregano. Pour in egg mixture and cook until set. Top with tomato mixture, Jarlsberg, basil and parsley. Cut into wedges and serve at room temperature.

ITALIAN SPINACH PIE

This stunning vegetable "torta," in the Italian vernacular, is superb warm or cold. It cuts into neat wedges for a party appetizer or first course, or makes a satisfying picnic entrée served paired with an herbed cheese dip, a basket of raw vegetables, grapes and biscotti.

WHOLE WHEAT EGG PASTRY

1 tsp. active dry yeast
1 tbs. lukewarm water
1 egg
¼ tsp. salt

1 tsp. olive oil
⅓ cup unbleached all-purpose flour
⅓ cup whole wheat flour

FILLING

2 medium onions, chopped
1 bunch green onions, chopped
2 tsp. olive oil
3 bunches spinach, or 2 bunches spinach
    and 1 bunch Swiss chard (about 3 lb.
    greens), chopped
3 cloves garlic, minced
8 oz. ricotta cheese

5 eggs, lightly beaten
salt and freshly ground pepper to taste
2 tbs. slivered fresh basil or sorrel
1 cup (4 oz.) shredded Romano or
    Parmesan cheese
12 basil sprigs, or slivered sorrel
    for garnish

For pastry, sprinkle yeast into water in a bowl and let stand until dissolved and puffy, about 10 minutes. Add egg, salt and olive oil and beat with a whisk until blended. Add flours and mix with a wooden spoon until smooth. Transfer dough to a lightly floured board, knead by hand for 1 to 2 minutes and shape into a ball. Cover dough with plastic wrap and let stand for 20 minutes before rolling.

Roll out dough to a 16-inch round and place in a 10-inch springform pan, letting dough cover bottom and sides of pan and drape over the edges by about 1½ inches.

Heat oven to 425°. In a skillet over medium heat, sauté onions and green onions in oil until limp. Add spinach and garlic and cook until spinach is wilted; press out any extra liquid. Transfer spinach mixture to a bowl and mix in ricotta, eggs, salt, pepper, basil and ¾ cup of the shredded cheese. Transfer mixture to pastry-lined pan and fold draping dough over filling. Sprinkle exposed filling with remaining shredded cheese. Bake pie for 15 minutes; reduce oven heat to 375° and bake for 15 minutes, or until eggs are set. Cool slightly before serving. Garnish each wedge with a basil sprig.

SPANISH POTATO OMELET

Servings: 4

Serve this hearty omelet hot for brunch or supper or at room temperature for a casual patio meal.

2 medium Yukon Gold potatoes
1 small onion, finely chopped
2 cloves garlic, minced
2 tsp. olive oil
4 eggs
salt and pepper to taste
dash hot pepper sauce, optional

2 tbs. minced fresh flat-leaf parsley, dill or basil
1/3 cup cooked small shrimp or oil-packed sun-dried tomatoes
flat-leaf parsley, dill or basil sprigs for garnish

Cook whole, unpeeled potatoes in boiling salted water until barely tender, about 15 to 20 minutes; drain potatoes, peel and slice about 1/4-inch thick. Heat broiler. In a large nonstick skillet, sauté onion and garlic in 1/2 tsp. of the oil over medium heat until soft. Beat eggs with salt, pepper and pepper sauce and mix in onion, potatoes, chopped herbs and shrimp or tomatoes. Heat remaining oil in skillet over medium heat and pour in egg mixture. Cook until eggs are set, shaking pan and lifting an edge to cook thoroughly and to prevent sticking. Place under broiler to set top.

At serving time, slide omelet onto a serving plate and garnish with herbs. Cool slightly and let guests cut their own wedges or squares.

SHELLFISH, FISH AND POULTRY

SHELLFISH PLATTER

Wine-steeped shellfish, zipped up with cilantro, were served to me in the seaport of Cascais, Portugal. A crisp vinho verde (Portuguese dry white wine) accompanied them, and for dessert, a ground almond cake with fresh peaches and whipped cream was luscious.

12 mussels, beards removed, or clams, scrubbed

12 scallops, preferably in their shells, scrubbed if necessary or muscles removed

12 medium shrimp

2 lobster tails, split, or 4 cooked crab claws

¾ cup dry white vermouth or dry white wine

⅓ cup minced fresh cilantro or flat-leaf parsley

3 cloves garlic, minced

2 tbs. unsalted butter

2 tbs. olive oil

lemon wedges

Place shellfish in a large pot with vermouth, 2 tbs. of the cilantro and garlic. Cover and simmer for 5 to 10 minutes, or until mussel or clam shells open. Discard shells that do not open. Transfer to a large platter and spoon juices on top. In a skillet, heat butter, oil and remaining cilantro until butter melts; spoon over shellfish. Garnish with lemon wedges. Accompany with dampened towels for cleaning hands.

SUGAR SNAP AND SCALLOP STIR-FRY

Accompany this delectable seafood stir-fry with hot steamed rice.

2 tbs. canola or peanut oil
2 green onions, with green tops, cut
  into 1/2-inch lengths
2 tsp. grated fresh ginger
1 clove garlic, minced
10 oz. scallops, muscles removed, or
  medium shrimp, peeled, slit
  lengthwise and deveined
1/2 lb. sugar snap peas or snow pea
  pods, trimmed

1/2 cup diced jicama or sliced water
  chestnuts
1/3 cup clam juice
1 tsp. cornstarch
1 tsp. cold water
1 tsp. soy sauce
dash hot pepper sauce, optional
2 tbs. minced fresh cilantro or sorrel
cilantro sprigs for garnish

Heat oil in a wok or large skillet over high heat. Add onions, ginger and garlic and stir-fry for 1 minute. Add scallops and stir-fry until scallops turn opaque. Add sugar snaps, jicama and clam juice and simmer for 1 minute, stirring. Blend together cornstarch, cold water, soy sauce and pepper sauce, if using, and stir into pan. Cook, stirring, until thickened. Sprinkle with minced herbs and garnish with cilantro sprigs.

SCALLOPS WITH SHALLOT AND BASIL SAUCE

Servings: 2-3 entrée, or 12 appetizer

Scallops make a superlative first course or an entrée, to sauté at the last minute. If you are lucky enough to get the "pink singing" scallops from Washington state, their artistic small shells make handsome serving containers for a pass-around appetizer.

3/4 lb. scallops
2 tsp. fresh lemon juice
1 tbs. olive oil
1 tbs. unsalted butter
3 shallots or green onions, white part only, minced

2 cloves garlic, minced
2 tbs. dry white wine or vermouth
2 tbs. unsalted butter
2 tbs. minced fresh basil
2 tbs. minced fresh flat-leaf parsley, chervil or chives

If using sea scallops, remove muscles and cut into quarters. Sprinkle scallops with lemon juice. In a large skillet, heat oil and 1 tbs. butter over medium-high heat and sauté shallots for 1 minute. Add scallops and sauté until browned on both sides, about 4 to 5 minutes. Add garlic, wine, 2 tbs. butter and basil, stirring to blend ingredients. Spoon into small scallop shells for appetizers or large shells or ramekins for entrées. Sprinkle with parsley.

GRILLED SCAMPI WITH HERBS

Servings: 4 entrée, or 18 appetizer

An elegant appetizer, first course or entrée features succulent scampi sealed in an herb-lemon glaze. Use either a barbecue or a broiler for cooking the shrimp.

3 tbs. lemon juice
1 tbs. dry vermouth
1 tbs. olive oil
2 cloves garlic, minced
1 tbs. minced fresh flat-leaf parsley
1 tbs. minced fresh dill or fennel

1 green onion, chopped
salt and freshly ground pepper to taste
1 lb. fresh extra-large shrimp (about 18 per pound)
chopped fresh dill, fennel or flat-leaf parsley for garnish

In a large bowl, mix together lemon juice, vermouth, oil, garlic, minced herbs, onion, salt and pepper. Peel shrimp, leaving tail shells intact, and split shrimp meat halfway to the tail; rinse out veins. Marinate shrimp in lemon juice mixture for 30 minutes.

Prepare a medium-hot barbecue fire or heat broiler. With soaked wooden skewers, spear shrimp just above the tail shell. Grill or broil, turning, for 4 to 5 minutes, or until shrimp turn pink and curl up in a butterfly shape. Garnish with herbs.

SHRIMP WITH MUSTARD-DILL SAUCE

Servings: 4

Cold shrimp in a zesty mustard sauce makes a delightful summer entrée for the patio or a picnic.

1½ tbs. dry mustard
2 tsp. Dijon mustard
2 tbs. dark brown sugar
1½ tbs. white wine vinegar
2 tsp. lemon juice
1 tbs. finely chopped fresh dill, or
   ¾ tsp. dried
salt and pepper to taste
1 tbs. canola oil

water
1 lemon, sliced
1 dried hot red chile
few seeds each allspice, mustard and
   coriander
1 bay leaf
1 lb. medium shrimp (about 32 per
   pound)

In a small bowl, combine dry and Dijon mustards, sugar, vinegar, lemon juice, dill, salt, pepper and oil and whisk together until blended. Cover and chill for several hours, preferably 24 hours, to blend flavors.

In a saucepan, place 2 inches of water and add lemon, red chile, seeds and bay leaf. Bring to a boil, reduce heat to low and simmer for 10 minutes to develop flavors. Add shrimp and simmer for 3 to 5 minutes, or until shrimp turn pink and opaque; drain and cool. Serve shrimp with small bowls of mustard-dill sauce for dipping. Let the guests peel their own shrimp.

CAPERED SOLE IN DILL-LEMON BUTTER

Servings: 2

Lemon, dill and capers give a fast uplift to fish fillets.

1 lemon
2 sole or turbot fillets, about 10-12 oz.
1 tbs. flour
salt and pepper to taste
2 tbs. unsalted butter or olive oil
1½ tbs. lemon juice
1 tbs. extra-large capers
2 tbs. minced fresh dill or sorrel

Cut ½ of the lemon into thin rounds for garnish. Peel remaining lemon half and chop lemon fruit into ¼-inch pieces. Coat fish very lightly with flour and season with salt and pepper. Heat a large skillet over medium-high heat, add 2 tsp. butter and sauté fish, turning to lightly brown both sides, for about 4 minutes, or until fish flakes with a fork. Transfer fish to a platter and keep warm. Add remaining butter to skillet and heat until butter turns golden brown. Add lemon juice, lemon bits and capers and stir to blend. Spoon sauce over fish, sprinkle with herbs and garnish with lemon slices.

SOLE IN AN HERB CLOAK

Servings: 2

A potpourri of sautéed fresh vegetables and herbs smothers quickly broiled fish.

2 sole fillets, about 10-12 oz.
salt and pepper to taste
2 tsp. lemon juice
1 tbs. plus 1 tsp. olive oil
¼ lb. white mushrooms, thinly sliced
2 green onions, chopped

1 medium tomato, peeled, seeded and
 diced
1 clove garlic, minced
2 tbs. minced fresh flat-leaf parsley
2 tbs. minced fresh basil

Heat broiler. Place fish fillets on a broiling pan, season with salt and pepper and sprinkle with lemon juice and 1 tsp. olive oil. In a large skillet, heat remaining oil over medium-high heat and sauté mushrooms, onions, tomato and garlic for about 1 minute, or until heated through. Stir in parsley and basil and remove from heat. Broil fish until golden brown, about 4 minutes (it is not necessary to turn it). Transfer fish to serving plates and spoon sautéed vegetables over the top.

FISH KEBABS TERIYAKI

Servings: 4 entrée, or 16 appetizer

Firm-fleshed fish, such as halibut, swordfish, mahi-mahi or salmon, is excellent to cut into chunks and grill for kebabs. The teriyaki marinade cooks to a golden-brown caramelized finish with a subtle sweetness.

1 lb. boneless halibut, swordfish, mahi-mahi, salmon or other firm-fleshed fish
2 tbs. dry sherry
2 tbs. soy sauce
1½ tsp. lemon juice or white wine vinegar

1 tsp. brown sugar
1 clove garlic, minced
2 slices fresh ginger, minced
1 tbs. canola oil
2 tbs. minced fresh cilantro or flat-leaf parsley

Cut fish into 1-inch pieces, removing skin and any hidden bones. In a bowl, combine sherry, soy sauce, lemon juice, sugar, garlic, ginger and oil; add fish pieces and stir well. Cover and chill for 2 hours, turning occasionally.

Prepare a medium-hot barbecue fire or heat broiler. Thread fish pieces on soaked wooden skewers and grill or broil for about 8 to 10 minutes, or until fish separates when tested with a fork. Baste occasionally with remaining marinade. Sprinkle with cilantro or parsley.

GREEK MARINATED FISH

White fish bathed in an aromatic herb, vinegar and olive oil bath is a savory encounter either hot or chilled. For a complementary accompaniment, serve chopped steamed sorrel dressed with olive oil.

1½ lb. shark, halibut or sole fillets
flour seasoned with salt and pepper
¼ cup extra virgin olive oil
¼ cup tarragon-flavored white wine vinegar
4 cloves garlic, minced
1 tbs. chopped fresh rosemary

Dip fish in seasoned flour, coating both sides lightly. In a large skillet, heat oil over medium-high heat and sauté fish, turning to brown both sides, about 4 to 5 minutes. Transfer to a warm platter. Add vinegar, garlic and rosemary to skillet, scraping up the drippings and cooking until liquid is slightly reduced. Spoon sauce over fish and serve hot or chilled.

ROASTED CHICKEN WITH HERBS AND GRAPES

Grapes explode with flavor after roasting in a plump bird.

3½ lb. broiler-fryer
2 cloves garlic, slivered
1 tbs. fresh tarragon leaves
1 tbs. fresh oregano or sage leaves
2 tbs. lemon juice
salt and pepper to taste

1½ cups seedless green or red grapes
2 tsp. grated fresh lemon peel (zest)
1 large onion, cut into ½-inch-thick slices
2 tsp. olive oil
½ cup water, or more if needed
⅓ cup dry white wine or vermouth

Remove innards and any excessive fat from chicken. Place garlic, tarragon and oregano under chicken breast skin. Drizzle chicken with lemon juice and season with salt and pepper. Toss grapes with lemon peel and tuck inside chicken cavity. Toss onion in oil and water and place in a large roasting pan. Place chicken breast-side down on a rack in pan and let stand at room temperature for 30 minutes.

Heat oven to 450°. Roast chicken for 20 minutes; turn chicken breast-side up and roast for about 30 minutes, basting with wine, until juices run clear when a thigh is pierced. Add additional water to pan if necessary to keep juices from browning too much. Pour off pan drippings and skim fat. Carve chicken into serving pieces and serve with grapes, onion and pan juices.

CHICKEN WITH ASPARAGUS AND LEMON SAUCE

A classic Greek entrée, chicken and egg-lemon sauce, gets a refined interpretation in this delicious pairing with fresh asparagus, mushrooms and herbs.

4 boneless, skinless chicken breast halves,
    about 1 lb.
salt and pepper to taste
1 clove garlic, minced
1 tbs. butter or oil
½ lb. small white mushrooms, halved if desired
2 tsp. minced fresh tarragon
⅓ cup dry white wine
½ cup chicken stock
¾ lb. slender fresh asparagus spears, ends trimmed
4 long fresh chives
2 cups prepared rice pilaf
Lemon Sauce, follows

Place chicken between 2 sheets of plastic wrap and pound lightly with a mallet to an even thickness. Season chicken with salt, pepper and garlic. In a large skillet over medium heat, sauté chicken in 1 tsp. of the butter or oil, until browned on both sides and cooked through, about 3 to 4 minutes; remove from pan and keep warm. Sauté mushrooms in remaining butter or oil just until softened; sprinkle with tarragon and remove from pan. Pour wine into pan and cook until reduced by half; add chicken stock and simmer for 2 minutes; reserve for sauce.

Steam asparagus until tender-crisp, about 5 to 7 minutes. Divide asparagus into 4 piles and tie each pile with a chive. Divide pilaf among 4 dinner plates, arrange a chicken breast alongside and place a bundle of asparagus over each portion. Spoon *Lemon Sauce* over asparagus and sprinkle with mushrooms.

LEMON SAUCE

Makes about 1 cup

½ cup pan juices
1 egg yolk
⅓ cup heavy cream or half-and-half

1 tbs. lemon juice
1 tsp. minced fresh tarragon

Pour pan juices into a saucepan and bring to a boil. In a bowl, beat egg yolk until light and stir in cream. Pour hot sauce into yolk mixture, stir to blend and return to saucepan. Cook over low heat until thickened, whisking constantly. Blend in lemon juice and tarragon just before serving.

GREEK ROASTED CHICKEN

Servings: 4-6

A golden bird and crispy brown potato sticks with a lemon tang make a succulent, easy entrée. Sweet, squishy roasted garlic lends an extra-special flair.

3½ lb. broiler-fryer
salt and freshly ground pepper to taste
4 large russet or Yukon Gold potatoes,
    peeled and cut lengthwise into
    ½-inch sticks

4 tsp. chopped fresh tarragon or oregano
1 large bulb garlic
1 tsp. olive oil
⅓ cup lemon juice
lemon wedges

Remove innards and any excessive fat from chicken. Season chicken with salt and pepper and sprinkle tarragon inside chicken cavity. Place chicken breast-side down on a rack in a large roasting pan and let stand at room temperature for 30 minutes.

Heat oven to 450°. Roast chicken for 20 minutes. Remove from oven and skim fat from pan drippings. Turn chicken breast-side up and add potatoes to pan around chicken, turning to coat in drippings. Cut base from garlic bulb and rub surface with oil; wrap with aluminum foil, place in a small baking dish and place in oven with chicken. Roast for 40 minutes, basting potatoes occasionally, until chicken and potatoes are cooked through. Pour lemon juice over chicken and transfer to a platter. Pour off pan juices and skim fat. Carve chicken into serving pieces, serve with potatoes and garlic cloves and offer lemon wedges to squeeze over chicken. Pass pan juices.

GRILLED TURKEY PATTIES WITH HERBS

Utilize fresh herbs from the garden or market to enliven everyday grilled burgers, prepared with either ground turkey or beef.

1¼ lb. ground turkey or lean ground
   beef
1 egg white
2 tbs. balsamic vinegar
2 shallots or green onions, minced

2 cloves garlic, minced
2 tbs. minced fresh flat-leaf parsley
salt and pepper to taste
Herb Dressing, follows

Prepare a medium-hot barbecue fire or heat broiler. In a bowl, mix turkey with egg white, vinegar, shallots, garlic, parsley, salt and pepper. Shape into 4 patties. Place patties on a rack and grill or broil until cooked through, turning once and allowing about 3 to 4 minutes per side. Transfer to plates and top with *Herb Dressing*.

HERB DRESSING

Makes about ½ cup

¼ cup minced fresh flat-leaf parsley
2 shallots, minced
2 tsp. minced fresh oregano or thyme

1 tsp. Dijon mustard
2 tbs. lemon juice

Mix all ingredients together in a bowl.

FLORENTINE MEATBALLS

Servings: 8

Ground turkey and turkey sausage lighten the traditional meatball, and spinach lends an added flavor dimension in this Italian-style version of meatballs.

1 bunch fresh spinach, or 1 pkg. (10 oz.)
   frozen chopped spinach, thawed
1 small onion, chopped
1 tbs. olive oil
1 egg
2 egg whites
¾ cup crumbled French bread
¼ cup minced fresh flat-leaf parsley

3 tbs. freshly grated Parmesan cheese
salt and freshly ground pepper to taste
1 tbs. chopped fresh oregano
3 cloves garlic, minced
1½ lb. ground turkey
½ lb. bulk turkey sausage
about 2 tbs. whole wheat flour for dusting
3 tbs. red wine vinegar

Wash and chop spinach, discarding stems. Place fresh spinach in a skillet and cook over high heat for 2 minutes, or until limp; drain well. Squeeze fresh cooked or thawed frozen spinach to remove as much moisture as possible. In a small skillet, sauté onion in 1 tsp. of the oil over medium heat until soft. In a large bowl, beat egg and egg whites and mix in bread, parsley, cheese, salt, pepper, oregano, garlic, meats, spinach and onion. Mix well to blend. Shape into 1-inch balls and dust with flour. Heat remaining oil in a large skillet over medium-high heat and sauté meatballs until browned on all sides and cooked through, about 4 to 5 minutes. Add vinegar and cook until reduced to a glaze, shaking pan to coat meatballs.

LEMON- AND HERB-BASTED TURKEY BREAST

A tangy lemon and fresh herb marinade perfumes roasted turkey for a year-round treat. This is excellent served either warm or chilled.

1 turkey breast, about 2½ lb., or 8
  chicken breast halves
juice and finely slivered peel (zest) of 2
  lemons
2 tbs. minced fresh rosemary
2 tbs. minced fresh oregano or marjoram
2 tbs. Dijon mustard

½ cup dry white wine
salt and pepper to taste
3 cloves garlic, minced
water, optional
rosemary sprigs for garnish
4-5 lemons, cut in half zigzag style,
  for garnish

Place turkey skin-side down in a baking dish. In a bowl, mix together lemon juice, lemon peel, herbs, mustard, wine, salt, pepper and garlic. Spoon ½ of the lemon mixture over turkey; cover and chill overnight.

Heat oven to 375°. Place turkey on a rack in a roasting pan. Roast turkey for about 1 hour, or chicken breasts for about 20 to 30 minutes, or until a meat thermometer registers 160° when inserted into the thickest part of meat. Baste with remaining marinade and, if necessary, add water to pan to keep pan juices from drying out. Serve on a carving board garnished with rosemary sprigs and lemon halves.

SKEWERED TURKEY OR VEAL ROLLS

Typically made with veal, turkey works admirably for a stylish entrée in these neat fast pinwheels.

1¼ lb. thinly sliced turkey breast or veal cutlets, about ¼-inch thick
3 tbs. Dijon mustard
3 oz. prosciutto, very thinly sliced
4 oz. fontina, Gruyère or Jarlsberg cheese

¼ cup minced fresh flat-leaf parsley
2 tbs. minced fresh oregano or sage
1 tbs. butter, melted, or olive oil
3 tbs. lemon juice
1 clove garlic, minced
freshly ground pepper to taste

Heat broiler. Cut turkey meat into 8 rectangles about 2½ x 5 inches. Lay turkey pieces flat on a board and spread lightly with mustard. Cut prosciutto and cheese into as many pieces as meat and lay a slice of each on top of meat. Sprinkle with parsley and oregano. Roll meat up jelly roll-fashion and thread on soaked wooden skewers, placing 4 on each skewer. Mix together butter, lemon juice, garlic and pepper and brush over each roll. Place skewers on a rack on a broiling pan. Broil about 4 to 6 inches from heat source until golden, turn and broil the other side, allowing about 4 to 5 minutes on each side to cook through.

MEATS

JOE'S SPECIAL

This scramble of ground beef or turkey, spinach and eggs is an old-time specialty from New Joe's North Beach Italian Restaurant in San Francisco. It makes a great spur-of-the-moment entrée.

2 green onions, with ½ of the green
   tops, chopped
¼ lb. white or brown mushrooms, sliced
1 tsp. olive oil
1 lb. lean ground beef or turkey
2 cloves garlic, minced
salt and pepper to taste

1 bunch spinach, stems removed, finely
   chopped
2 eggs
2 tbs. shredded Romano or Parmesan
   cheese
2 tbs. minced fresh chives
1 tbs. minced fresh oregano

In a large skillet, sauté onions and mushrooms in oil over medium-high heat until soft. Push to the side of skillet, add ground beef, garlic, salt and pepper and cook until meat is browned. Mix in spinach and cook for 2 minutes, just until spinach wilts. Break eggs over mixture and stir until mixed and cooked through. Sprinkle with cheese, chives and oregano.

HAWAIIAN MEATBALL AND FRESH PINEAPPLE KEBABS

The explosive refreshment of tart-sweet pineapple and gingery spiced meatballs fills the palate in this island combination.

1 lb. lean ground pork or turkey
1½ tbs. low-sodium soy sauce
1 tbs. dry sherry
1 tsp. minced fresh ginger
2 cloves garlic, minced

1 green onion, with ½ of the green
   top, finely chopped
16 chunks fresh pineapple
2 tbs. minced fresh cilantro
Chinese plum sauce or chutney

Prepare a medium-hot barbecue fire or heat broiler. In a bowl, mix together ground meat, soy sauce, sherry, ginger, garlic and onion. Shape mixture into ¾-inch balls. Thread meatballs alternating with pineapple chunks on small soaked wooden skewers, leaving room at one end for a handle. Grill or broil skewers about 4 inches from heat source, turning frequently, for about 7 minutes, or until meat is cooked through. Arrange skewers on a heated platter, sprinkle with cilantro and serve with plum sauce or chutney for dipping.

TURKISH LAMB MEATBALLS

These spicy Turkish meatballs are excellent hot or tepid, served with a squeeze of lemon juice or a yogurt-dill dip.

1 lb. ground lamb
1/3 cup chopped red onion
3 cloves garlic, minced
1 tbs. pine nuts
1 tsp. cinnamon, or 1/2 tsp. ground
   cumin
2 slices bread, rubbed into crumbs
1 egg

1/4 cup minced fresh flat-leaf parsley
2 tbs. minced fresh dill, optional
salt and freshly ground pepper
flour for coating
1 tbs. olive oil
lemon wedges or yogurt seasoned
   with minced garlic and dill

In a bowl, mix meat with onion and garlic. Mix in nuts, cinnamon, breadcrumbs, egg, parsley, dill, if using, salt and pepper. Shape into 1-inch balls and roll in flour. In a large skillet, heat oil and sauté meatballs, turning to brown all sides and cooking until medium-rare*, about 4 minutes. Serve with lemon wedges or seasoned yogurt.

*Some health authorities discourage eating undercooked meat because of possible bacterial contamination.

PESTO BEEF PATTIES

This flavor-packed variation on fillets with mushroom crowns features ground round for a budget-wise, yet classy entrée.

10 oz. beef ground round
1/4 cup *Oregano Pesto*, page 22, plus
    more for filling mushroom caps
2 large mushroom caps
1 tsp. olive oil
1 tsp. balsamic vinegar

Mix ground round with 1/4 cup *Oregano Pesto* and shape into 2 patties about 3/4-inch thick. Chill for 1 hour to blend flavors.

Prepare a medium-hot barbecue fire or heat broiler. Brush mushroom caps with oil and vinegar. Grill or broil mushrooms and meat patties for about 2 to 3 minutes per side for mushrooms and 3 to 4 minutes per side for beef*. Place patties on plates, top with mushrooms, cup-side up, and fill caps with additional pesto.

*Some health authorities discourage eating undercooked meat because of possible bacterial contamination.

MEAT LOAF CORDON BLEU

A striping of cheese, prosciutto and parsley bisects this flavorful meat loaf for an all-season's winner, from a tasty summer picnic entrée to a winter repast.

1 bunch green onions, chopped
½ tsp. olive oil
¾ cup soft white French or Italian breadcrumbs
3 tbs. dry sherry
⅓ cup chicken stock
3 egg whites
½ tsp. salt
freshly ground pepper to taste
1 tbs. Dijon mustard
1 tbs. balsamic vinegar
2 cloves garlic, minced
⅓ cup minced fresh flat-leaf parsley
1 lb. lean ground beef or turkey
1 lb. lean ground pork
¾ cup (3 oz.) shredded Jarlsberg or Emmentaler cheese
1 oz. prosciutto or ham, thinly sliced
2 tbs. minced fresh sage or thyme

Heat oven to 350°. In a medium skillet over medium heat, sauté onions in oil until soft. With a blender or food processor, blend breadcrumbs, sherry, stock, egg whites, salt, pepper, mustard, vinegar, garlic and ¼ cup of the parsley until smooth. Place ground meats in a bowl, add breadcrumb mixture and mix until blended. In an oiled 9-x-13-inch baking pan, pat out ½ of the meat mixture into a rectangle about 6 x 10 inches. Mix together sautéed onions, cheese, prosciutto, remaining parsley and sage and sprinkle over meat. Pat out remaining meat mixture on a sheet of plastic wrap, forming another 6-x-10-inch rectangle. Invert meat rectangle over cheese and ham filling, remove plastic wrap and press edges of meat layers together, forming a compact loaf. Bake for 1 hour, or until cooked through. Serve while still warm or chill and serve sliced.

TACO CASSEROLE

For a potluck or party dinner, assemble this vibrant Mexican-style casserole in advance. Apropos accompaniments are sangria, guacamole salad, hot rolled tortillas and a fresh pineapple, melon and strawberry platter.

1 tbs. olive oil
2 medium onions, finely chopped
2 inch cinnamon stick
1 lb. ground pork
1 lb. ground turkey
2 cloves garlic, minced
2 cans (8 oz. each) tomato sauce
2 tbs. red wine vinegar
1/2 tsp. ground cumin
1/2 tsp. chili powder
1/2 tsp. dried oregano

salt and freshly ground pepper to taste
1 can (16 oz.) dark kidney beans, drained
1 pkg. (6 oz.) small corn chips
2 cups (1/2 lb.) shredded Monterey Jack cheese
2 green onions, chopped
1 bunch fresh cilantro, stems removed, chopped
3/4 cup plain yogurt or sour cream

In a large skillet, heat oil over medium heat and sauté onions and cinnamon stick until onions are soft. Add ground meats and sauté until browned. Stir in garlic, tomato sauce, vinegar, cumin, chili powder, oregano, salt and pepper. Reduce heat to low, cover and simmer for 30 minutes. Stir in beans; remove cinnamon stick.

Layer ⅓ of the corn chips in an oiled 2-quart casserole. Sprinkle with ⅓ of the cheese. Cover cheese with ½ of the meat sauce. Add another ⅓ of the corn chips and ⅓ of the cheese and top with remaining meat sauce. Top with remaining corn chips and cheese. If desired, chill casserole at this point.

Heat oven to 375°. Bake casserole for 20 minutes (40 minutes, if refrigerated), or until heated through. Toss green onions and cilantro together and make a border around top of casserole. Spoon yogurt into the center.

SESAME BEEF STRIPS

Servings: 4 entrée, or 16 appetizer

You can barbecue these meat strips over charcoal or cook them in a frying pan. Look for mu shu wrappers in Asian markets.

1 lb. top round steak
2 tbs. low-sodium soy sauce
1½ tsp. red wine vinegar
1 clove garlic, minced
2 tsp. minced fresh lemon grass or
  lemon balm
freshly ground pepper to taste
1 tsp. minced fresh ginger

1½ tsp. sesame seeds, toasted and
  crushed
1-2 tsp. olive oil
dash hot pepper sauce
1 shallot or green onion, chopped
16 small mu shu wrappers
about 1 bunch cilantro sprigs
plum sauce

Cut meat across the grain into very thin slices about 3 inches long. In a bowl, mix together soy sauce, vinegar, garlic, lemon grass, pepper, ginger, sesame seeds, 1 tsp. of the oil, pepper sauce and shallot. Add meat strips and mix well. Chill for 3 hours or longer.

Prepare a medium-hot barbecue fire, if desired, and grill meat for about 1 minute on each side. Or, heat 1 tsp. oil in a large nonstick skillet over medium-high heat and sauté meat in a single layer, cooking quickly on both sides. Warm wrappers in a microwave for a few seconds or wrap with aluminum foil and heat in a 350° oven for 10 minutes. Place a meat strip, a cilantro sprig and a spoonful of sauce inside each wrapper and roll up to eat.

BEEF FILETS WITH
MUSHROOM-PESTO CROWNS

Finish off grilled filets in great style with a jaunty mushroom cap bearing pesto.

2 beef filets, about 5 oz. each
2 large shiitake mushrooms, stemmed
   or brown mushrooms
1 tbs. lemon juice
2 tbs. balsamic vinegar
1 tbs. olive oil

1 shallot, finely chopped
1 clove garlic, minced
salt and freshly ground pepper to taste
1/4 cup *Sun-Dried Tomato and Roasted*
   Garlic Pesto, page 23

Place meat and mushrooms in a locking plastic bag. Mix together lemon juice, vinegar, oil, shallot and garlic and toss with meat mixture. Seal bag and marinate in the refrigerator for 2 hours or longer.

Prepare a medium-hot barbecue fire or heat broiler. Grill or broil mushrooms and meat for about 2 to 3 minutes per side for mushrooms and 3 to 4 minutes per side for medium-rare beef*. Season with salt and pepper. Place filets on plates, top with mushrooms, cup-side up, and fill mushrooms with pesto.

*Some health authorities discourage eating undercooked meat because of possible bacterial contamination.

BEEF STEAK VINAIGRETTE

Marinated steak and mushrooms are ideal picnic fare for a make-ahead warm weather entrée.

1 jar (6 oz.) marinated artichoke hearts
1/4 cup olive oil
1 tbs. lemon juice
1 tbs. white wine vinegar
3 tbs. dry vermouth
1 shallot, chopped
salt and freshly ground pepper to taste

2 tsp. minced fresh marjoram
2 tsp. minced fresh thyme
1/3 lb. white or brown mushrooms, sliced
1 lb. sirloin or flank steak, broiled and chilled, or leftover beef roast
1 cup halved red and gold cherry tomatoes for garnish

Drain marinade from artichoke hearts into a bowl and mix with oil, lemon juice, vinegar, vermouth, shallot, salt, pepper, marjoram and thyme. Cut artichoke hearts into bite-sized pieces and mix with mushrooms and marinade; chill for at least 30 minutes. Thinly slice steak across the grain and arrange slices overlapping on a shallow serving dish. Spoon marinated vegetables and marinade over steak. Cover and chill. Garnish with halved tomatoes at serving time.

CRETAN PORK AND POTATOES

A canopied outdoor taverna at the charming resort of Aghios Nikolai on the Greek island of Crete offered this tantalizing stew in individual fat clay pots.

2 lb. boneless pork, veal or beef stew
   meat
1 tbs. olive oil
1 large onion, finely chopped
2-inch cinnamon stick
6 whole cloves
4 cloves garlic, minced
salt and freshly ground pepper to taste

2 cups water
3 tbs. tomato paste
1/4 cup white wine vinegar
6 small new red or Yukon Gold
   potatoes, cut in half
2 tbs. mixed minced fresh thyme, sage
   and flat-leaf parsley
1/2 cup (2 oz.) grated Romano cheese

Heat oven to 325°. Cut meat into 1½-inch cubes. In a flameproof casserole or saucepan, heat oil over medium-high heat and sauté meat until browned on all sides. Add onion and cinnamon and cook until onion is soft. Place whole cloves in a tea ball or tie in a small square of cheesecloth; add to meat mixture with garlic, salt, pepper, water, tomato paste, vinegar and potatoes. Stir to blend and bring to a boil. Cover casserole and bake for 1½ to 2 hours, or until meat is fork-tender. Remove spices. Sprinkle casserole with herbs and cheese.

VEAL-STUFFED MUSHROOMS

Servings: 4 entrée, or 16 appetizer

Oversized mushrooms, about 3 inches across, offer flavor-packed containers for a meaty stuffing. Serve as an entrée, first course or appetizer.

16-18 large brown mushrooms, about
   3 inches in diameter
1 small onion, chopped
1 carrot, shredded
2 tsp. olive oil
2 tbs. minced fresh flat-leaf parsley
1 tbs. minced fresh oregano or thyme
1 clove garlic, minced
¾ lb. ground veal or turkey

salt and freshly ground pepper to taste
¼ tsp. nutmeg
2 oz. chopped prosciutto or ham
¼ cup fine dry breadcrumbs
½ cup (2 oz.) grated Parmesan cheese
½ cup chicken stock
¼ cup dry white wine
minced fresh flat-leaf parsley for garnish

Heat oven to 375°. Remove mushroom stems and chop. In a skillet, sauté onion and carrot in 1 tsp. of the oil over medium-high heat until limp; add chopped mushroom stems and sauté just until heated through. Place in a bowl and mix with parsley, oregano and garlic. Sauté meat in remaining oil until browned and season with salt, pepper and nutmeg; add to vegetables. Mix in prosciutto, breadcrumbs and cheese. Lightly pack mixture into mushroom caps. Arrange caps in a baking dish and pour in stock and wine. Bake for 25 minutes, or until mushrooms are cooked through and filling is lightly browned. Serve warm garnished with parsley.

SWEET BREAKFAST DISHES AND DESSERTS

FRENCH GALETTE WITH LEMON BALM BERRIES

This pizza-like sweet bread goes together swiftly and bakes in a flourish. Serve it warm, shortcake-style, with fresh berries and cream for a spectacular breakfast dish or dessert. Substitute sliced peaches or nectarines for a delicious variation.

1 pkg. active dry yeast
6 tbs. warm water
1/4 cup unsalted butter, room temperature
2 tbs. sugar
1 egg
1 1/2 tsp. coarsely grated fresh lemon peel (zest)
1/2 tsp. salt
about 1 2/3 cups unbleached all-purpose flour
2 tbs. butter, softened
1 tsp. cinnamon
3 tbs. sugar
2 cups mixed raspberries, blackberries and blueberries
1 tbs. minced fresh lemon balm
sour cream or berry-flavored frozen yogurt, optional

In a large bowl, sprinkle yeast into water and let stand until dissolved and puffy, about 10 minutes. With a heavy duty mixer or wooden spoon, beat in 1/4 cup butter, 2 tbs. sugar, egg, lemon peel and salt. Gradually add enough flour to make a soft dough (you may not need to use all of it) and beat well. Transfer dough to a lightly floured board and knead until smooth and satiny. Place dough in a lightly oiled bowl, cover with plastic wrap and let rise until doubled in size, about 1 1/2 hours.

Punch down dough, transfer to a lightly floured board and knead lightly. Roll out dough to a 15-inch round and place on an oiled 14-inch pizza pan or baking sheet. Form a rim around the edge. Spread dough with 2 tbs. softened butter. Mix together cinnamon and 3 tbs. sugar and sprinkle over butter. Let stand in a warm place for 20 minutes until slightly risen.

Heat oven to 500°. Bake galette for 6 minutes or until crust is golden brown. Serve warm, using scissors or a pizza wheel to cut into wedges. Accompany with berries tossed with lemon balm and a dollop of sour cream or frozen yogurt.

DUTCH BABY WITH RASPBERRIES AND LAVENDER-ORANGE CREAM

This puffy pancake gets an intriguing topping of lavender-spiked orange cream and fresh berries. You can also substitute blueberries and blackberries and/or garnish with sliced nectarines or peaches.

3 eggs
¾ cup milk
1 tbs. plus 1 tsp. honey
1 tsp. grated fresh orange peel (zest)
¾ cup all-purpose flour
¼ cup plain yogurt

¼ cup sour cream
3 tbs. frozen orange juice concentrate, thawed
2 tsp. fresh lavender blossoms
2 cups raspberries or hulled and halved strawberries

Heat oven to 425°. With a blender or food processor, blend eggs, milk, 1 tbs. honey, orange peel and flour until smooth. Pour into an oiled 9-inch round baking dish. Bake for 20 minutes, or until puffed and golden brown.

While pancake is baking, stir together yogurt, sour cream, orange juice concentrate, lavender and 1 tsp. honey and transfer to a serving bowl. Spoon berries into another bowl. Serve hot pancake with berries and lavender-orange cream spooned over the top.

APRICOT STREUSEL COFFEECAKE

A spicy caramel cake puffs up between the tangy apricots for this "oh so good" breakfast torte to dollop with honey-lemon yogurt cheese. Substitute other fruits of the season for year-round pleasure.

1/4 cup plus 2 tsp. butter
1/3 cup plus 2 tbs. brown sugar, packed
2 eggs, separated
1/2 tsp. vanilla extract
2/3 cup plus 2 tsp. all-purpose flour
1 tsp. grated fresh orange peel (zest)
1/4 tsp. salt

6 apricots or plums, halved, or 3
　nectarines or pears, peeled and sliced
1/2 tsp. cinnamon
1/3 cup chopped almonds
1/2 cup *Yogurt Cheese*, page 16
2 tsp. minced fresh lemon balm
1 tsp. honey

Heat oven to 375°. In a bowl, cream 1/4 cup butter with 1/3 cup brown sugar until light. Beat in egg yolks and vanilla. Stir together flour, orange peel and salt and mix with butter mixture. In a bowl, beat egg whites until soft peaks form and fold into batter. Spread in an oiled and floured 10-inch tart pan with a removable bottom. Arrange fruit on top, cavity-side up. In a bowl, mix together 2 tbs. brown sugar, 2 tsp. flour, 2 tsp. butter, cinnamon and almonds until crumbly and sprinkle over fruit. Bake for 25 minutes, or until cake is golden brown and fruit is tender. Serve warm or cooled, cut into wedges. Accompany with *Yogurt Cheese* flavored with lemon balm and honey.

FRUIT-FILLED CREPES

For a Sunday brunch or summer dessert, warm berry-filled crepes, dolloped with lemon cream, provide a regal treat. For ease, make the crepes in advance to reheat at the last minute.

2 eggs
1 tbs. granulated sugar
1/4 tsp. salt
2/3 cup milk
1/2 cup all-purpose flour
1 tsp. vanilla extract
1 tbs. butter
3 cups mixed raspberries, blueberries and blackberries, or sliced peaches or
   nectarines
2 tbs. confectioners' sugar
1/3 cup light sour cream
1 tsp. minced fresh lemon balm or lemon-flavored mint

Blend eggs, sugar, salt, milk, flour and vanilla with a blender or food processor until smooth. Let batter stand for at least 30 minutes to 1 hour.

Heat a 6-inch crepe pan over medium heat and add 1/4 tsp. of the butter. When butter stops sizzling, pour in about 2 tbs. batter, tilting pan to cover surface with batter. Cook until golden brown underneath, turn and cook the opposite side. Transfer crepe to a plate and repeat the cooking process with remaining batter. Stack crepes, cover with plastic wrap and chill if made ahead.

Heat oven to 300°. Toss berries or peaches with confectioners' sugar and spoon about 1/4 cup of the fruit down the center of each crepe; roll up and place in a baking dish. Bake filled crepes for 10 minutes, or until heated through. Serve 2 crepes to each person and dollop with sour cream blended with lemon balm or mint.

ROSEMARY BUNDT CAKE

Servings: 16

This golden pound cake with a cornmeal crunch is imbued with the woodsy hint of rosemary. Cut into thin slices and serve with whipped cream and mixed berries for a sumptuous dessert.

1 cup unsalted butter, softened
2 cups sugar
4 eggs
1 tbs. grated fresh lemon peel (zest)
1 cup yellow cornmeal
2¼ cups all-purpose flour
2 tsp. baking powder
½ tsp. baking soda
¾ tsp. salt
1 cup plain yogurt
⅓ cup sugar
⅓ cup water
2 tbs. chopped fresh rosemary
1 tbs. lemon juice
½ tsp. vanilla extract

Heat oven to 350°. Butter and flour a 10-inch Bundt pan. In a large bowl, beat butter and sugar with an electric mixer until light and fluffy. Add eggs and lemon peel and beat until blended. Stir together cornmeal, flour, baking powder, soda and salt and add to egg mixture alternately with yogurt, beating until combined. Transfer mixture to prepared pan and bake for 1 hour and 5 minutes, or until a tester inserted into the cake away from an edge comes out clean.

In a small saucepan, simmer 1/3 cup sugar, water, rosemary and lemon juice for 5 minutes. Remove from heat and stir in vanilla. Cool syrup for 30 minutes and strain through a sieve.

Cool cake in pan on a rack for 10 minutes. Invert onto a serving platter and, while still warm, drizzle with cooled syrup. Cut into wedges to serve.

PEAR CRISP WITH LAVENDER WHIPPED CREAM

Lavender-scented cream accents tender pears in this homey crisp.

¼ cup butter, room temperature
⅓ cup all-purpose flour
¾ cup sugar
⅓ cup coarsely chopped walnuts or pecans
4 all-purpose pears, such as Bartlett, Anjou or Bosc
¾ cup heavy cream
2 tbs. fresh lavender blossoms
2 tsp. confectioners' sugar

Heat oven to 350°. Mix together butter, flour, ½ cup of the sugar and nuts until crumbly. Peel and slice pears, toss with remaining ¼ cup sugar and transfer to an oiled 1½-quart baking dish. Spread crumb mixture evenly over top. Bake for 30 minutes, or until topping is browned.

Whip cream with lavender and confectioners' sugar until soft peaks form. Serve warm crisp with flavored whipped cream.

LEMON GRASS SOUFFLÉ CUSTARD

A soufflé topping caps this tart custard pudding.

1 cup milk
1 tsp. minced fresh lemon grass
1 tsp. minced fresh ginger
3 tbs. flour
⅔ cup sugar
2 eggs, separated

2 egg whites
¼ tsp. salt
¼ tsp. cream of tartar
2 tbs. butter, melted
1½ tsp. grated fresh lemon peel (zest)
⅓ cup lemon juice

In a small saucepan, heat milk with lemon grass and ginger until hot; cool and let stand for 20 minutes. Strain milk, discarding lemon grass and ginger. Heat oven to 350°. In a small bowl, mix flour with ¼ cup of the sugar. Beat 4 egg whites until foamy. Add salt and cream of tartar and beat until stiff, but not dry; beat in remaining ¼ cup sugar. In another bowl, beat egg yolks until thickened. Add sugar-flour mixture, melted butter, lemon peel, lemon juice and flavored milk. Fold egg white mixture into egg yolk mixture. Spoon into buttered individual soufflé dishes or other small baking dishes. Place in a baking pan containing 1 inch hot water and bake for 20 to 25 minutes, or until set.

GINGER THYME CRISPS

Fresh thyme and spicy ginger enhance these buttery wafer cookies that simply melt in your mouth. Their fragile texture is due to the unique leavening ingredients.

1 cup butter, softened
2 cups confectioners' sugar
1 egg
2 tbs. grated fresh lemon peel (zest)
2 tsp. minced fresh thyme, preferably
  lemon thyme

1 tbs. minced fresh ginger
2½ cups all-purpose flour
1 tsp. baking soda
1 tsp. cream of tartar
½ tsp. salt
2 tbs. confectioners' sugar

In a large bowl, cream butter with 2 cups confectioners' sugar until light. Beat in egg, lemon peel, thyme and ginger. Stir together flour, baking soda, cream of tartar and salt and mix into butter mixture, beating until just combined. Divide dough in half and, on separate sheets of waxed paper, form each half into a 12-x-1½-inch log. Chill until firm, or freeze for about 20 minutes.

Heat oven to 350°. Cut dough into ⅜-inch-thick slices and place on parchment-lined or ungreased baking sheets. Bake for 10 to 12 minutes, or until edges are golden brown. Dust tops of cookies with 2 tbs. confectioners' sugar shaken through a sieve.

LAVENDER ORANGE SORBET

Fresh lavender lends a heady, haunting scent to this tangy, bright-colored ice. It is lovely paired with a small scoop of rich vanilla bean ice cream for contrast.

1 tbs. grated fresh orange peel (zest)
2/3 cup sugar
2/3 cup water
3 tbs. fresh lavender blossoms
2½ cups fresh orange juice
¼ cup lemon juice

Mash orange peel with 1 tsp. sugar to bring out orange oils. Combine remaining sugar and water in a saucepan with lavender and bring to a boil, stirring to dissolve sugar. Cook until syrup is clear; remove from heat and cool. Strain syrup and stir in orange juice, lemon juice and orange peel. Chill thoroughly. Freeze according to the directions for your ice cream maker. Or, pour prepared mixture into a 9-inch square pan. Cover with aluminum foil or plastic wrap and freeze until firm, about 2 to 3 hours. Scrape out frozen mixture and transfer to a food processor workbowl or the bowl of an electric mixer. Process or beat until light and fluffy, but not thawed. Transfer mixture to a freezer container, cover and freeze until firm, about 1 to 2 hours.

STRAWBERRY MINT SORBET

Serve this scarlet sorbet in balloon-shaped wine glasses with a few berries for a dazzling dessert.

¾ cup sugar
¾ cup water
1½ qt. strawberries, hulled
3 tbs. lemon juice
2 tbs. chopped fresh mint or lemon balm

Combine sugar and water in a small saucepan. Bring to a boil and cook until sugar dissolves, about 3 minutes; cool. Puree berries, lemon juice and mint with a food processor or blender. Stir in sugar syrup and chill thoroughly. Freeze according to the directions for your ice cream maker. Or, pour prepared mixture into a 9-inch square pan. Cover with aluminum foil or plastic wrap and freeze until firm, about 2 to 3 hours. Scrape out frozen mixture and transfer to a food processor workbowl or the bowl of an electric mixer. Process or beat until light and fluffy, but not thawed. Transfer mixture to a freezer container, cover and freeze until firm, about 1 to 2 hours.

LEMON GRASS WINE ICE

This taste-tingling ice enhances a Thai or Far-Eastern menu. Serve it as a dessert or a refresher between several small courses. Select a fruity wine, such as a Semillon-Sauvignon Blanc, dry Chenin Blanc or Gewurztraminer to compliment the sour-lemon gingery flavor of lemon grass. In a temperate climate, stalks of lemon grass are easy to root and grow in the garden. Mine are available for cutting year-round.

three 6-inch stalks fresh lemon grass	¾ cup sugar
2½ cups dry white wine	¾ cup water
½-inch piece fresh ginger, chopped	2 tbs. fresh lemon juice

Peel lemon grass and cut into 1-inch lengths. In a saucepan, combine lemon grass with wine and ginger and bring to a boil; remove from heat and let stand for 30 minutes. In another saucepan, combine sugar and water and cook until syrup is clear; cool to room temperature. Strain wine mixture, discarding lemon grass and ginger, and stir into sugar syrup; add lemon juice, cool and chill thoroughly. Freeze according to the directions for your ice cream maker. Or, pour mixture into a 9-inch square pan. Cover with aluminum foil or plastic wrap and freeze until firm, about 2 to 3 hours. Scrape out frozen mixture and transfer to a food processor workbowl or the bowl of an electric mixer. Process or beat until light and fluffy, but not thawed. Transfer mixture to a freezer container, cover and freeze until firm, about 1 to 2 hours.

MINT ICE CREAM WITH CHOCOLATE LEAVES

*This refreshing ice cream has several options for an elegant garnish. You can paint mint leaves with chocolate for a candy accompaniment or serve each bowl with **Hot Fudge Sauce** drizzled over the ice cream.*

2 cups milk
¼ cup chopped fresh mint, packed
6 egg yolks
¾ cup sugar
2 cups heavy cream
3 oz. bittersweet chocolate, melted, optional
several fresh mint leaves, optional
Hot Fudge Sauce, follows, optional

In the top of a double boiler over hot water, heat milk and mint until steaming; let stand for 15 minutes and puree with a blender. In a medium bowl, beat egg yolks slightly and stir in sugar and mint-infused milk. Transfer mixture to top of double boiler, place over hot water and cook, stirring constantly, until thick enough to coat a spoon, about 10 minutes. Remove from heat and cool in a pan of ice water. Chill until cold and strain, discarding mint leaves. Stir in cream. Freeze according to the directions for your ice cream maker.

To make chocolate leaves, brush melted chocolate over mint leaves, place on a foil-lined pan and chill until set; peel mint from chocolate leaves and discard mint.

Serve ice cream in dessert bowls and garnish with a few chocolate leaves or drizzle with *Hot Fudge Sauce*.

HOT FUDGE SAUCE

Makes about 1 cup

4 oz. bittersweet chocolate, chopped
$\frac{1}{3}$ cup half-and-half
3 tbs. corn syrup
$\frac{1}{2}$ tsp. vanilla extract

Place chocolate, half-and-half and corn syrup in the top of double boiler. Heat over hot water, stirring, until smooth and heated through. Stir in vanilla.

MELON BERRY COMPOTE

Mingle a medley of berries and melon for a refreshing summer treat.

2 cups cubed cantaloupe or Crenshaw
  melon
½ cup fresh raspberries
½ cup fresh blueberries
⅓ cup orange juice

2 tbs. fresh lime juice
2 tbs. honey
2 tsp. finely minced fresh lemon grass
  or mint
lemon balm or mint sprigs for garnish

Combine all ingredients, except herb sprigs, in a bowl. Toss gently, cover and chill. Serve garnished with herb sprigs.

RUBY FRUIT COMPOTE

As this compote chills, the berries exude their juices, turning the citrus syrup scarlet.

juice and grated peel (zest) of 1 orange
juice and grated peel (zest) of 1 lime
¼ cup sugar
2 cups watermelon balls

1½ cups strawberries, hulled
½ cup raspberries
1 cup seedless red grapes or blueberries
mint or lemon balm sprigs for garnish

In a saucepan, boil juices, peels and sugar, stirring until sugar is dissolved; cool and chill. Pour chilled syrup over fruit in a bowl, cover and chill for 2 to 3 hours or longer, stirring gently once or twice. Serve garnished with herb sprigs.

STRAWBERRY APRICOT BOWLS

Servings: 4

Showcase the season's prime fruit with simplicity at its best.

2 cups hulled and quartered strawberries
1½ cups sliced apricots
3 tbs. honey

1 tbs. slivered fresh lemon balm
frozen vanilla yogurt or frozen praline
   yogurt for garnish

In a bowl, toss together berries, apricots, honey and lemon balm; cover and chill. Serve in wine goblets or dessert bowls and top with frozen yogurt.

RHUBARB AND STRAWBERRY BOWLS

Servings: 4

The fresh tang of raw rhubarb and tarragon is a scintillating accent with berries for a light dessert. It's a favorite from a country restaurant in Honfleur, France.

2 stalks rhubarb, finely diced, about
   ⅔ cup
2 cups hulled and sliced strawberries
2 tbs. honey

1 tsp. minced fresh tarragon
1 tsp. grated fresh lemon peel (zest)
frozen vanilla or raspberry yogurt for
   garnish

In a bowl, combine rhubarb, berries, honey, tarragon and lemon peel. Let stand at room temperature for 1 hour to blend flavors. Serve in dessert bowls topped with a scoop of frozen yogurt.

FRUIT PLATE WITH LEMON GRASS-ORANGE CREAM

A ginger-spiked creamy custard gilds a plateful of fruit to serve at the end of a meal. Vary the fruit with whatever is in season.

2 egg yolks
2 tbs. honey
1/4 cup orange juice
1 1/2 tbs. fresh lime juice
2 tsp. grated fresh ginger
2 tsp. minced fresh lemon grass
1/2 cup heavy cream
2 kiwi fruit, peeled and sliced

1 1/2 cups strawberries, hulled
2 red Bartlett pears, cored and sliced, or 2 bananas, sliced
1 small papaya, peeled, seeded and sliced, or 2 oranges, peeled and thinly sliced
1/4 cup thinly sliced crystallized ginger

In the top of a double boiler, beat egg yolks until light; beat in honey, orange juice, lime juice, ginger and lemon grass. Cook over hot water, stirring, until thick enough to coat a spoon, about 15 minutes. Remove from heat and immediately place over a pan of ice water and let stand until cold; push through a sieve to remove ginger and lemon grass fibers. Whip cream until soft peaks form and fold into egg yolk mixture. Transfer to a serving bowl. Arrange fruit on dessert plates in a decorative pattern. Spoon cream in the center of each plate and sprinkle with crystallized ginger.

INDEX

SERVE CREATIVE, EASY, NUTRITIOUS MEALS WITH nitty gritty® cookbooks

Fresh Vegetables
Cooking With Fresh Herbs
The Dehydrator Cookbook
Recipes for the Pressure Cooker
Beer and Good Food
Unbeatable Chicken Recipes
Gourmet Gifts
From Freezer, 'Fridge and Pantry
Edible Pockets for Every Meal
Cooking with Chile Peppers
Oven and Rotisserie Roasting
Risottos, Paellas and Other Rice
    Specialties
Muffins, Nut Breads and More
Healthy Snacks for Kids
100 Dynamite Desserts
Recipes for Yogurt Cheese
Sautés
Cooking in Porcelain
Appetizers
Casseroles
The Toaster Oven Cookbook
Skewer Cooking on the Grill
Creative Mexican Cooking
Marinades
The Wok

No Salt, No Sugar, No Fat Cookbook
Quick and Easy Pasta Recipes
Cooking in Clay
Deep Fried Indulgences
Cooking with Parchment Paper
The Garlic Cookbook
From Your Ice Cream Maker
Cappuccino/Espresso: The Book of
    Beverages
The Best Pizza is Made at Home
The Best Bagels are Made at Home
Convection Oven Cookery
The Steamer Cookbook
The Pasta Machine Cookbook
The Versatile Rice Cooker
The Bread Machine Cookbook
The Bread Machine Cookbook II
The Bread Machine Cookbook III
The Bread Machine Cookbook IV:
    Whole Grains and Natural Sugars

The Bread Machine Cookbook V:
    Favorite Recipes from 100 Kitchens
The Bread Machine Cookbook VI:
    Hand-Shaped Breads form the
    Dough Cycle
Worldwide Sourdoughs from Your
    Bread Machine
Entrées From Your Bread Machine
The New Blender Book
The Sandwich Maker Cookbook
Waffles
The Coffee Book
The Juicer Books I and II
Bread Baking
The 9 x 13 Pan Cookbook
Recipes for the Loaf Pan
Low Fat American Favorites
Healthy Cooking on the Run
Favorite Seafood Recipes
New International Fondue
    Cookbook
Favorite Cookie Recipes
Cooking for 1 or 2
The Well Dressed Potato
Extra-Special Crockery Pot Recipes
Slow Cooking

For a free catalog, write or call:
Bristol Publishing Enterprises, Inc.
P.O. Box 1737
San Leandro, CA 94577
(800) 346-4889
in California (510) 895-4461